Proof?

Does God Exist?

By Philip Gardiner

Proof? Does God Exist?

By

Philip Gardiner

Artwork by
Philip Gardiner

Radikal Phase Publishing House
Willow Court
Cordy Lane
Underwood
Nottinghamshire
NG16 5FD
England
www.radikalbooks.com

A catalogue record for this book is available from the
British Library. ISBN 1 904126 01 4

Printed and bound in England by the
Phase Group, Willow Court, Cordy Lane, Underwood,
Nottinghamshire, Ng16 5FD. UK
Tel: 01773 764288 Fax: 01773 764288
Web: www.phaseprint.com

Contents

Introduction

"If a man will begin with certainties, he shall end in doubts; but if he will be content to begin with doubts, he shall end in certainties.", Francis Bacon, 1561-1626.

If you have bought this book then you are asking questions. These same questions have been asked for thousands of years - by the first Shaman and Medicine men of primitive cultures, to the high philosophers of the Hellenised world. With each passing generation we are no closer to the truth of whether god exists.

What does change is our perception of what this god is or should be. In the beginning we may have held the gods or god to be Animistic, Totemic or even plain agricultural deities. Attributing all manner of special and wonderful meanings to their persona. In many instances astrological or astronomical ideologies were placed over these early beliefs. This gave real life to the flames, light and heat of the sun, resurrecting nightly the cold light of the moon.

Religious structures give a sense of power and permanence.

Our systems developed and evolved as we learned more and more about the world around us. Eventually we became more rational and literal. At a unique period of time the gods were themselves rationalised into just one all encompassing god, which just happened to be male. Of course this was after the destruction of the idea of the balancing goddess, Sophia. She has been hidden within the Gnostic surviving traditions as Mary, Isis and various other female deities. For the literalists this female counterpart or Lilith, was simply in the way and we were left with one, male god. This god, because he was the accumulation of all the ideas and symbols of the other deities also held all the answers to all our questions. A super god.

This one super god could have emerged from anywhere at any time, had that time been right. But the time was right in the Middle East. There was a vacuum and an Empire sufficiently placed to help this new way grow. Eventually this new faith manifested itself around the globe as Christianity. After this eruption of new ideology and with the world rapidly becoming a smaller place it became increasingly less likely that any other monotheistic religion would ever be quite as successful. Any successor would have to wage war with the might of Christianity. This is one of the reasons I have chosen to keep the focus of this book more towards Christianity rather than say, Islam or Buddhism.

There has, however, been a war raged, as we all know. Not just a physical battle of the strongest but also a more subtle psychological battle of propaganda. This makes sifting through the evidence more difficult than it would otherwise be, due to the layers of lies and deceit always present when propaganda is utilised.

With this in mind and using history as a tool we can only forecast a balancing out of beliefs and a coming together of world religions. The opposite is almost too bloody to bear. Hopefully a rationalism of this long-term propaganda will fuse the minds of these otherwise intelligent people.

For now we have to use the evidence at hand to decide for ourselves what the truth is. We can take no relevance or help from how intelligent a believer or non-believer may be. There are many millions of highly intellectual people who hold to the faith of either god or atheism. We cannot say that just because a Professor believes in god then we should also. There are a many great reasons for the emotional state of belief. And that is exactly one of them. Belief and faith are emotional states, not intellectual property. Something inside of us is said to demand an answer. Something, possibly part of an evolutionary instinct, emits a strong desire for there to be more to life than that which we have. Many believe this to be part of the cyclic problem, that we have a beginning and an end, and we cannot deal with this. As if to circumnavigate the problem we give our gods the ability to resurrect, just as do the sun and moon and stars daily and nightly. We then claim this as a gift from our god, that we may also be miraculously resurrected.

The sheer terror of there actually being an end to life is often too much for us to bear and religion has the answer. Now, in this modern age, we also cling to other more peculiar belief systems such as Alien worship and seeing the Universe as a living organism. These become easier to believe due to the perceived rationalism behind them. In time these ideologies will alter into something else we cannot even imagine.

In all things we need balance, careful consideration and an analytical mind to help us see beyond the emotional states of not just ourselves but others also.

So just what is the purpose of religion?

Is it god's answer to the questions man cannot answer? Or is it simply man's answer to those same questions?

In this book we are looking for the answer to two questions. What or Who is god? And what are we to understand represents proof?

Firstly then to god. What is the Christian point of view?

God is our concept of the Supreme Being. The creator, lord and manager of our lives. He made everything. He is omnipotent, all seeing and all knowing, the beginning and the end. We cannot hide from god. He is to be worshipped for all he has done for us. He is to be petitioned in prayer and we are to place faith in him for all our needs. He is our saviour, taking away all our sins so that we can reconcile ourselves again with him.

We cannot, yet, explain god in scientific terms. Whoever does will make a lot of money. There are moments of quantum understanding that one day may bring us close, but however close we do get, it will still be a million miles off the mark.

Humans are finite beings; we are still, after all this time trying to understand what must be an infinite being, if indeed he exists.

We, as finite beings, look for a beginning and an end. The Bible even tells us that god is the Alpha and Omega (the first and last letters of the Greek alphabet). Life must start somewhere and end somewhere; we simply cannot understand it any other way.

Yet, if we were gods, we would possibly exist in some 4th dimensional state that mere humans simply could not comprehend. We would know everything, in all time, all at once, present, past and future. We would hold the power to create life and take it away again. To choose life or death for billions is the kind of power only mad men dream of.

That is why we would also be love. According to the Bible, god Is love. This would be just as well. The power to create and destroy life needs the taming of love.

Hopefully now we have a better understanding of what many Christians believe to be god.

So what about proof?

Proof is evidence that something is true. But how do we know what is true? It can be two ways. For instance I am a white man, and yet I am also a sort of pink colour. Which is true. Both are obviously true. One is true symbolically and one true literally. These are the truths we have to sift through when reading the Bible or any other ancient tradition or myth.

I cannot prove to you that Shakespeare wrote Hamlet, it is something we have faith in. There is evidence that Marlowe also had a hand in many of Shakespeare's works. What is true? There has been many thousands of researchers look into this mystery and still no hard evidence has emerged. How much more important then is it that we discover the author or authors of the Bible? Was it man or god?

Philip Gardiner
UK

Prophetic or pathetic

Prophecy can be a very powerful way of showing that the Bible / Koran is the word of god. Many theologians argue that some Bible prophecies were written after the event however, and point to prophetic self-fulfilment.

For Christians prophecy ensures the strengthening of faith as Peter wrote, "..and we have the word of the prophets made more certain, and you will do well to pay attention to it, as to a light shining in a dark place, until the day dawns and the morning star rises in your hearts. " 2 Peter 1: 19. When  we begin to take a deeper look into Biblical prophecy we find ourselves startled at the immense scope and the intricately detailed DNA-like structure that it weaves through the centuries. Surely if there is a god, and that is the question of this book, and if that god is the Biblical god, we must believe that he gave us his word through prophets, men of his word. However, to be totally fair we must look at other, non-Biblical fortune telling, for in doing so we should be able to discern the differences between the prophecies of god and the childlike grasping of man. This in itself can be used as strong 'evidence' for the existence of god, albeit circumstantial. The very range of subject matter is both bewildering and ridiculous. Of the following you will surely have heard of a few: - Divination, clairvoyance, augury, astrology, horoscopy, palmistry, crystal gazing, dowsing, and tarot card reading.

Prophet or Profiteer?

From Biblical days monarchs have seen fit to employ so-called prophets and seers. Even in our contemporary age the illustrious leaders of western and some eastern countries employ people to read their horoscopes or palms and tell them whether to have a hair cut or press the big button. Many stars and personalities join in with "New Age" fortune telling and end up making stars and personalities out of the fortune-tellers, who then, make huge amounts of money. Each week in many countries we now have Astrology television programmes, telling us our fortunes and listening to the wonderful coincidences week in and week out.

Back in the sixteenth century much the same thing was happening with the rulers of England. The prophet of the day was a man named John Dee (1527-1608) who, although failing to predict the death of King Edward VI correctly, was employed for a time by Queen Mary, in order that she may "have her and her husbands horoscopes read."

Dee fell in with a man named Edward Kelly who claimed to see spirits in crystals and held long conversations with dead people. Things did not turn out well for Dee when a spirit called Madimi told Kelly that Dee should share his wife with him.

Dee, a spy of the realm and also known as 007, was taken in by a trickster. Kelly can be shown to have deceived Dee. Together they managed to manipulate dozens of Royalty including the Polish King and Holy Roman Emperor. It was the clever workings of a government spy and a superb con man in the guise of Kelly that managed to be the talk of Europe. Eventually Dee lost his home in England and became almost secondary to the legend of his previous underling Kelly. In the end there is no proof that any of the Dee/Kelly scenario is true prophecy from spirits or god. It is in actual fact a sad story of deceit.

In the fifteenth century a woman by the name of Janet Ursula Southiel, now commonly known as Mother Shipton, supposedly predicted the Great Fire of London in 1666AD and the English Civil War.

Even at birth rumours of "the Devils child" and "Lucifer's daughter" were abound and her mother was accused of copulating with the Devil. Her mother vanished to a convent and a nurse took Ursula in as her own. Ursula went on to marry Tobias Shipton and moved from Knaresborough to Skipton.

However, any keen historian upon closer inspection will find that the prophecies are so obscure that they could mean anything from making telephone poles to the invention of satellite dishes. With the advance in science and technology, interpretations of Mother Shipton's prophecies are updated still by her ardent followers to fit with the times in which we live. Take for example the following rhyme which, has since been "attributed" to Mother Shipton, and therefore 'becomes' hers:-

Carriages without horses shall go,
And accidents fill the world with woe,
Around the earth thoughts shall fly,
In the twinkling of an eye;
The world upside down shall be,
And gold found at the root of a tree,
Through the hills man shall ride,
And no horse shall be at his side,
Under water men shall walk,
Shall ride, shall sleep, shall even talk,
In the air men shall be seen,
In white, in black, in green,
Iron in the water shall float,
As easily as a wooden boat,
To an end the world shall come,
In the year two thousand and sixty one.

Sounds wonderfully authentic doesn't it? She must have been in touch with god himself. No, afraid not. This magnificent rhyme of doom was created centuries after her time and attributed to her. Were you wondering over the words? Were you imagining the telephone as being the thoughts flying around the earth? This is how we are sucked into believing. A little at a time, with words placed into the mouths of prophets. Now after all this time it is hard for the onlooker to discern between fact and fiction. Did she really predict the Great Fire of London? Highly unlikely.

The same is true of Michel de Nostradame or Nostradamus, who has lately taken an upsurge in popularity. He is from the same period as Mother Shipton and again much of his work is attributed to him and may not even be his, let alone from his period. Also his words are most often so obscure as to be able to be interpreted in any way at all. He supposedly predicted the death of the French King Henry II, but again it is concealed in such cryptic language that it only serves to give it a taste of the mythological and surreal. This is basically why the work of Nostradamus can be re-released every century because it will always find a subject matter with which the vagaries of his language can adapt.

From profit and fame, attention-seeking individuals, sincere mystics, and just plain fools, we turn now to a totally different aspect of prophecy. Richard Brothers (1757-1824) surprisingly anticipated the death of King Louis XVI. He then went on to claim that he was a direct descendant of King David and the nephew of the almighty. Needless to say, whatever spirits Richard Brothers had been listening to were probably out of a bottle. Eventually he was committed to an asylum and declared insane.

We may laugh and mock the people of ages past, but are we any better? In fact we seem to be worse. At least our ancestors had the excuse of low technology and lack of information. What is our excuse?

Are there simply too many problems with prophecy to use it as proof? There are no live witnesses, no scientific analysis and simply too many other reasons for people to create the myth. Whoever uses prophecy as a proof for the existence of some higher being is simply perpetuating that myth. And yet Christianity maintains this element as part of its weaponry for conversion. How does this weaponry hit the target? Why are we still affected by prophecy? Indeed, why do we seek predictions?

Horror-scopes!

Today 91% of people read their star signs which only leaves 9% that do not. This of course means that people of all faiths are also doing so. Of this 91% who do read them, 70% read stars for fun and 20% really believe them. Eight million people read their horoscopes daily in newspapers. This is just a hint at how big this business is.

Historically it all began some three thousand years ago (and highly likely more - see The Shining Ones by same author), with Babylonian priests. They watched the night sky and noted the seven wanderers that turned out to be the planets (less the obvious ones that were discovered later). They then divided this heavenly map into first thirteen segments then twelve, and used it as a kind of calendar.

A few people were chosen and their birth days logged, then they were closely watched and their traits of anger, loyalty, patience and so on were carefully written down. This is where the equations used today originated.

Even if those big rocks out there in space could somehow guide our life and help us make decisions we would be making the wrong decisions now. The star signs are exactly one month out from when they were firsts created. So whatever star sign you think you are, you're not.

People still joyously go ahead even today and lay out the Tarot cards and truly trust in the upturned pictures of chance. They will watch the mass of twinkling stars in the "heavens" and put money down on their now ever so sure futures. With upturned palms people are preyed upon by professional fair ground Machiavellian storytellers. And yet it is easier for the sake of our conscience to not believe in god, to go on enjoying ourselves in iniquity, but deep down we seem to have a need to be sure of the future, of why we are here.

Take a look outside your window. There may be trees and plants or maybe you live in a city and all you see are buildings and concrete. Wherever you live, you will notice one thing. There is, even at our level, a massive amount of order. The trees have branches and leaves, all with wonderful symmetry. In the concrete landscape we see man's interpretation of our own in-built order. The precise number of windows, the angles, the colours, all balanced.

This wonderful order follows through, in everything, from the grass we walk on, to the stars in the sky. The much credited chaos theory has little to do with the order we are talking about here. In fact the chaos theory merely backs up the balance of life and its almost thermodynamic order. There is even a mathematical underlying symmetry to chaos theory which has recently been proven by scientists. Chaos really is unrecognisable order.

So what is the meaning of all this order? Why is the universe so ordered? Why do we have symmetrical bodies, hands, feet, arms etc? This question cannot be answered without putting a meaning into existence - the all-important question, what is the meaning of life? This eventually leads us to a belief that order has been created, that order came from chaos.

This question has tormented mankind ever since we could walk and talk. Yet, even now, in this scientific age we still have the questions unanswered. Is it in fact unanswerable? Is there simply no meaning to life? And why do we have such a hard time believing that? Are we simply just walking bags of chemicals and water that have come together just perfectly over millions of years? Or is there some great universal law and plan behind all of this? After all, we seem to be comfortable with anything when we can tie it down with a law or two. Every generation seems to come up with new laws and theories and so our reality alters from what it was to what it is. When the Romans invaded Britain we were worshipping pagan Sun Gods and Moon Gods amongst a pantheon of deities. Now WE have a different reality, changed vastly over a long period of time. Gradually we have taken the answers away from deities and found them in science and rationalism.

And yet, science still cannot provide the answers to the very fundamental questions at the root of all life. Why are we here? What is it all about? Who or what started it all and why? And so again we keep coming full circle, asking the same questions without answers.

Will we find a balance some day? A balance between spirituality and science? There does seem to be something very special about being human. Our knowledge that we are alive. We must ask, is there a reason for this? Will we find, as some Christians say, that the spiritual element of our life cannot be explained scientifically. They explain their experience as if god was broadcasting a radio signal and they had to tune into him. Sometimes, they say, the signal is confusing and all they get is static. But other times they get a clear signal and really understand god. Maybe mankind has forgotten how to tune himself in. Maybe god is still broadcasting to a reducing audience?

Many people do say that their minds were more aware and in a higher state of consciousness when they became Christian. Is this because they finally tuned in their signal? Or is it a chemical and psychological reaction to the religious experience? Finding a natural state of bliss?

Two thousand years ago in the arid desert of the Middle East, Hebrew priests and prophets wandered around issuing forth proclamations of truth from god. Radio messages of the future. Their reality was very different to ours today. There were far fewer other signals around blocking those of god, if indeed there were any. Maybe Bible prophecy is the evidence for that signal having been picked up all those years ago? And then again, maybe it is just as flawed as the other prophets of the globe.

Bible Prophesy

"For I will give you words and wisdom that none of your adversaries will be able to resist or contradict.", Luke 21:15.

Let us look at the prophet Isaiah, who, writing in around 700 BC, apparently accurately predicted the following:-

"Who says of Cyrus, "He is my shepherd and will accomplish all that I please"; he will say of Jerusalem, "Let it be rebuilt" and of the Temple, "Let its foundations be laid"", Isaiah 44:28

When Isaiah supposedly wrote this, there was no such King as Cyrus, Jerusalem was fully built and the Temple was standing. However, 100 years after writing these fateful words the city and Temple were destroyed by King Nebuchadnezzar in 586 BC. After this it was taken by the Persians in 539 BC and their King, named Cyrus, gave a decree to rebuild, as in Ezra 1:2, "This is what Cyrus King of Persia says: "The Lord, the god of heaven has given me all the Kingdom of the earth and has appointed me to build a Temple for him in Jerusalem in Judah."" (See also Chronicles 36:22)

So Isaiah apparently prophesied a whole 160 years before the event with a name, a place and what would happen. That is of course if we believe Isaiah.

Herodotus the fifth century Greek historian records that the Euphrates was diverted from running through the centre of Babylon by Cyrus in order to allow his Persian army to enter under the walls by means of the riverbed. This proves that there was such a person as Cyrus, at the correct time, took the Babylonian Empire and incorporated Jerusalem.

Of course there are numerous accounts of the exploits of King Cyrus, even his own words say, "I also gathered all the former inhabitants and returned them to their habitations." He was of course speaking of the return of the people of Judah from Babylon, itself a fulfilment of other Bible prophecies.

Now what about Nebuchadnezzar? In Jeremiah 15:8 we read, "I have brought upon them against the mother of the young men a spoiler at noonday: I have caused them to fall upon it suddenly, and terrors upon the city." Which if we were to take the word "mother" to mean Jerusalem or metropolis of the land, the passage might then read, "I have brought against the Mother City a spoiler at noonday". However in chapter 21:7 he speaks in straight language leaving no doubt, "After that, declares the Lord, I will hand over Zedekiah King of Judah, his officials and the people in the city who survive the plague, sword and famine, to Nebuchadnezzar King of Babylon and to their enemies who seek their lives."

Now all this is very interesting, especially when we consider that Jeremiah was supposedly writing this at least thirty-four years before the actual event. Daniel confirms the truth of the event in Daniel 1:1, "In the third year of the reign of Jehoiakim King of Judah, Nebuchadnezzar King of Babylon came to Jerusalem and besieged it."

In the book of the minor prophet Nahum we find the foretelling of the downfall of Nineveh. Lo and behold we now find in the chronicles of the Babylonian King Nabopolassar that indeed the combined forces of the Chaldeans and Medeans did actually destroy Nineveh in 612 BC. In fact it was so devastated that Xenophon did not even recognise it as the site of a city when he passed in 401 BC.

Continuing the theme we find Joel, another minor prophet in the Biblical sense predicting a major Christian event, "I will pour out my spirit on all people, your sons and daughters will prophesy, your old men will dream dreams, your young men will see visions." If we then read Acts 2:14 onwards we see this wonderfully self-fulfilling at Pentecost, when god apparently pours out his spirit on the gathered Apostles.

In the New Testament we see John the Baptist also self-fulfilling Old Testament prophecy. Isaiah said "A voice of one calling; "In the desert prepare the way for the Lord; make straight in the wilderness a highway for god."" In John 1:23 this self-fulfilling prophecy is seen with "I am the voice of one calling in the desert, "Make straight the way for the Lord."" Of course it was that now famous foreknowledge of Jesus that John was talking about.

On the face of it all this prophecy is tremendous stuff. All this predicting must surely be from god. Well lets carry on a little and look at the most famous prophecies - the amazing 300 plus prophecies of Jesus.

Prophecy - Virgin Birth
Isaiah 7:14 "The virgin will be with child and will give birth to a son, and will call him Immanuel." Which means god is with us and is derived from Egypt.

Fulfilment
Luke 1:26-32. The angel tells the Virgin Mary that she will "be with child and give birth to a son."

Virgin Birth Notes: - Virgin Birth and cave instances in birth - Isis immaculately conceives Horus. Virgil said the messiah would be born of the Virgin Lady. Zoroaster was born of a virgin. Abraham in a cave. Muhammad enlightened in a cave. Jesus given birth to in a cave. Fatima the Shining One gave birth to three sons and is said to have been a virgin. In China the Virgin birth consists of treading in the footprint of god which the mother of Hou Chi did and was born like a 'lamb'. He was born amidst sheep and cattle just like Jesus. (Hou sounding like the Great Hu or Shining Light and part of JesHu [Jesus])

There are of course many religions that had this prediction. Zoroaster was born of a virgin on December 25th. It was a basic Shamanic tenet.

Prophesy - Born in Bethlehem.
Micah 5:2, "But you, Bethlehem Ephrathah, though you are small among the rulers of Judah, out of you will come for me one who will be ruler over Israel, whose origins are from old, from days of eternity."

Fulfilment
Luke 2:1-7, Joseph and Mary go apparently to Bethlehem because of the census and Mary gives birth to a son.

It is very much disputed now that Bethlehem even existed at the time. Mary was in a cult of the Virgins, hence the title, created around prophecy and ancient and traditional religious practices. For more information see The Shining Ones.

Prophecy - Seed of Abraham
Genesis 22:18, "...and through your seed all nations on earth will be blessed."

Fulfilment

Matthew 1:1, "A record of the genealogy of Jesus Christ the son of David, the son of Abraham..." Well if we are to believe that Abraham was the "father of nations" then we are all his sons and anybody could then be the one to blessed.

These are just a few samples. There are over 300 more, which Christians have been using for 2000 years to convince the world of their belief. They say that even Christ himself predicted his own death and resurrection. Well, if he had planned it with his fellow conspirators, as many now believe then of course he could have predicted it. Even so, the New Testament was written after the event and could have easily been made to fit with the facts. And unfortunately the same is true of all Bible prophecy. There is absolutely no evidence to suggest anything other than self-fulfilling and fictitious writing has occurred.

And then there are those Bible prophecies still to come true.

We are lead to believe that Christ will return and "On that day, his feet will stand on the Mount of Olives, east of Jerusalem, and the Mount of Olives will be split in two from east to west." Strangely geologists have discovered a geometric fault line running east to west right through the Mount of Olives. Could Zechariah have known this without scientific evidence? Or is it really proof for the existence of god? Of course we will not really know until Jesus returns and splits the mountain in half. Of course when he does I will personally eat my hat and a few more besides.

In Zechariah 14:12 speaking of the day of the Lord, "This plague with which the Lord will strike all the nations that fought against Jerusalem: Their flesh will rot while they are standing on their feet, their eyes will rot in their sockets and their tongues will rot in their mouths."

Sounds like nuclear war or even biological or chemical warfare, something unknown when written. Every generation since the text was written has said the same thing. Plague, small pox or any manner of wonderfully unhealthy phenomena. Are you convinced yet? This is some of the best evidence Christianity has; you should be signing up to the Salvation Army by now.

Let's continue.

Now Christians point at the mathematical probability of all the prophecies of Jesus to be true. It goes like this: -

For all the prophecies concerning the crucifixion to have come true on the same day, to the same person, from writings by 60 different men, who never even knew each other (an assumption), were from totally different backgrounds (now being disproved) and were written over a period of 1400 years would work out to be one in one hundred billion.

But then, it is now the belief of many that; Jesus was part of a long ranging and powerful plots to implement a new religion. That he fulfilled prophecy "on purpose" for various reasons. That these people were not from different backgrounds and were in fact trained under the same roof and that their very simple titles of "fishermen" etc are in actual fact religious titles. To be a fisherman was simply to be a converter of men to the faith or Baptiser. Now the mathematical improbability becomes highly likely.

So the prophecies in this old book are convincing to many but none of it would stand up in court and many of the prophecies could be interpreted in many thousands of ways. This is the major problem with any religious text and therefore it simply cannot be taken as proof for god. We need instead scientific hard evidence in mathematical possibility and probability. We need modern day convincing we are wiser now, we need more than riddles interpreted by biased believers. Yes Jesus, I am afraid we do now need to see the holes in your hand.

Bible Code

So now, what about the famous Bible Code? This is possibly, one of the most astounding discoveries of mankind, or simply one of the most astounding inventions of mankind. It appears to be an in built prophecy, which has been locked within the structure of the Bible for thousands of years. The peculiar thing is that it is only now, in our modern computer literate age that we are able to decipher the code.

In the beginning of his book, The Bible Code, Michael Drosnin quotes Albert Einstein as saying "The distinction between past, present and future is only an illusion, however persistent."

A not unusual philosophical statement for a scientist of Einstein's ilk, who worked hard on some quite profound scientific theories. And yet Einstein was human too and free to theorise about god like the rest of us. The quotation however sums up the Bible Code quite well. Maybe it is all an illusion, however persistently provable the maths may be. Using some extremely clever mathematics, it appears there may well be something unexplainable within the hidden depths of the Bible.

We have to temper our judgement by remembering who is behind the discovery of the Bible Code. Michael Drosnin is a respected journalist. Doron Witztum, Eliyahu Rips and Yoav Rosenberg are all respected Jewish mathematicians. These are clever people with a lot of respect. However we have to wonder, because of their faith, whether they have a vested interest in ensuring that the Bible continues to be utilised by the worlds Jews. Michael Drosnin however still fails to come to a belief in god, even with all the evidence he displays. He remains a little short of blaming it all on aliens.

I have read the book, and the other books, which duly followed, I have done the maths and yet I still cannot bring myself to believe the Bible Code as a prophecy from god.

There is not enough space in the pages of this book to outline all the evidence for the Bible Code however I can say that further research into the esoteric, hermetic and ancient alchemical traditions show some remarkable similarities in structure. The Jews had specific methods of copy writing material with in built mathematical structures to ensure perfect copies. This in turn gives the effect of a purposely-structured text, built around a peculiar written language, which can be read in many different ways.

I would however seriously advise anybody to read the book and make up his or her own mind.

So just how does this famous code work?

Firstly and importantly, only the book of Genesis was checked. In Statistical Science 1994 Vol 9, No 3, 429-438, Witztum, Rips and Rosenberg put forward their case for the Equidistant Letter Sequences in the book of Genesis. Originally discovered by Rabbi Weissmandel who found "interesting" patterns in the five books of Moses.

Taking Weissmandel's discovery further the three mathematicians went on to prove that by choosing equidistant letter sequences in the text, not counting spaces, they found that the letters spelt out words with related meanings. For example "Yitzhak Rabin" and "assassin that will assassinate", "Amir", "In 5756" (Hebrew year for 1995), "Tel Aviv" and Rabin Assassination", were all found hidden in the depths of a book written thousands of years before the actual assassination did take place by a man called Amir in Tel Aviv in 1995.

Also included are the assassinations of Kennedy, both of them, Anwar Sadat and many more. In fact according to Drosnin probably everybody on the planet is in there somewhere. It all seems amazing. Indeed, so amazing that I have been waiting for his follow up book, "My Famous Hoax".

The problem is that there seems to be very few serious and none religious mathematicians and scholars interested in getting to the bottom of this "probability factor". It is my belief that this is simply down to the language, the structure of copying and our modern day interpretation, seeing what we want to see. This kind of structure is extremely difficult to find in English as there are very few of our words which actually have different meanings. In the language of Genesis we almost have a religion created language that has many meanings. Apply a mathematical structure to the text, any mathematical structure, and you will find something.

This is one of those kinds of evidence that is almost too amazing to be true. Maybe we are simply finding what we want to find. Or maybe god is actually giving us some clues.

Bogus Beliefs

No book about the proof of the existence of god can be written without some reference at least to world religion. Indeed nor should it. For by investigating the many and varied beliefs of man, we can highlight one truth at least. Mans relentless search. From the beginning man has sought after god. He has built great monoliths at the dawn of his age, buried riches and tools with him in preparation for the next life and sacrificed animal and human to appease the mighty gods. Does this not reveal man's need to Know? His craving for reason? Why do I exist? What purpose can my life have? Where am I going after this?

Even distinguished so-called atheists, are so-called because they have made some kind of search and found, for themselves nothing. Take Darwin for instance and his theory of evolution. When his last days came and his maker called, he cried out for the local Gospel Hall attendant and choristers in order that he might repent of his misgivings.

Most of us when pushed to the very limits of our beings call out for help, be it in a war situation, close to death or psychological need. Why is this? If we are so sure that god does not exist, why do we, and in our deepest need call out to him? Is it because within us there is an empty space, a void caused when we walked away from god? Or is it, as some say, an evolutionary thing, a totally natural process and we all have to fill our own void as we mature? Now in the confusion of a multitude of faiths and non-faiths we search and strive to either, get back to god or discover peace, once again to find that 'lost age' which mankind supposedly once knew.

In the following pages you will see the various ways in which man has tried to get back to god. It is my hope that in comparing mans attempts at explaining what life is all about, we shall see if any one shines out as being true. On the one hand, maybe letting his imagination run riot and inventing all kinds of rituals that meet his needs and on the other maybe god.

When we look at the world's religions it is as though we are seeing them through a cloudy mist. Mankind has heaped so much mystery onto the basics that we are no longer looking at that, which was meant to be. Take Christianity for example, now to many almost a dirty word, bringing to mind such things as the struggles in Northern Ireland and the so-called Holy Crusades. But when we look at the founding fathers we see a peaceful tradition trying to grow. So what happened?

We need to address this issue strongly from the beginning as it can cause much misunderstanding. We need to look back and see just what did the originators say and do. On this basis only, should we make our stance, not on what is now perceived of the specific religions? We must not take for instance, what the Bishop of Durham says is the Gospel, but take only the Gospel as gospel. (Not forgetting that the same applies for all religions)

The following study has been approached upon this basis, taking only those religions that are deemed historically and spiritually relevant enough to obstruct truth or maybe obviously are the truth. Of the abundance of religions available to us I have chosen the two largest (other than Christianity), using the conclusion at the end of the section to pick up on a few points from the other, smaller faiths or cults.

Please keep in your thoughts (while reading these religious answers) the questions you would have for a god and try to recognise that thing called the "Ring of truth". Remember also that if god has made himself known to us then one of the "religions" of the world could be right. Can we afford therefore, to ignore what these religions have to say? .

Buddha or Bible?

The Buddhism of today has deep and varied roots that according to tradition began around 600 BC with the birth of a young man by the name of Siddhartha Gautama.

His father, called Suddhodana was Rajah of a small principality at the foot of the Himalayas and was married to a woman called Maya. These respectable, high classed parents wanted their son to become the future heir and Rajah. As Suddhodana had awaited the birth of the child he traditionally said, "The love of a son cuts into the skin; having cut into the skin it cuts into the flesh, the ligaments, the bones; having cut into the bones it reaches the marrow." But his son was not meant for Rajah status, as such things are too worldly for a future holy man.

Many myths have become attached to, and enveloped the true story of Gautama, making his actual history almost impossible to trace. Much like the tales of Robin Hood or King Arthur which we know are based on certain truths, but alas have been clouded in the mysteries of mans romantic imagination. It must be pointed out that the two aforementioned tales are much younger historically and thus ought to have more factual connotations attached to the stories. This I hope gives you some idea as to the difficulty of gaining actual facts about this man who lived around 600 BC, came from a small provincial area and claimed mystical enlightenment.

There are few on the ground witnesses, little or no contemporary history, (apart from supposed writings by a few disciples that have very little scholarly backing) and scriptures which came a whole 400 years after his death, all making Buddhism a step of great faith. However when one talks to Buddhists one finds a lack of concern for proof and historical facts. They are more concerned, and rightly so, about their spiritual growth and living a compassionate life. They are very relaxed and concerned people, however they are still human, and being this are open to all the same temptations as the rest of us, they also succumb to these temptations like the rest of us. Therefore this religion, like all the others, does not set its people apart.

However, based on such writings and scriptures that we do posses I will endeavour to find certain events for the historically minded among us.

According to the traditional writings it seems Gautama wanted very much to find happiness, both for the people and his own inner self. Having found it, he would then pass it on, so that others might receive it also.

At that time and in that area the spiritual leaders preached that the road to happiness was through asceticism (not allowing oneself pleasures or luxuries), and thus Gautama joined this path by following one called Alara Kalarma who taught the "consciousness of nought". After having discovered all he could learn about "nothing" Gautama moved on to follow Uddaka who taught "neither perception, nor non-perception ". Which must have been equally enlightening.

It was broadly recognised in India at this time that asceticism lead to happiness because by starving oneself, beating oneself and generally wearing down the body one allowed the true spirit to emerge. Gautama tried all this and found it wanting. Having discovered that asceticism was not the road to "True Reality" he eventually found "Release from the Weariness of Existence" whilst sitting under a Bo tree near the River Gaya. It should be acknowledged that this was the meditative culmination of years of searching and is probably only symbolic, but nevertheless it may have been where Gautama finally changed his mind or had the revelation that beating oneself was not the way. The tree is also highly symbolic from a shamanistic point of view. The World tree holds knowledge and is the key to the wonders of Heaven.

Anyhow he was suitably enlightened, and having discovered that the root to all evil was greed and desire, he preached a wonderful compassion, not only for mankind but also for all living things.

He said that the common and noble, beautiful and ugly, happy and sorrowful would all have their souls depart at death. However if you are evil in words and thoughts then you will go to a mental hell. Whereas the ones who live right and think right shall enter a heavenly realm. This was the original Righteous Order of the Universe or Cosmic Law Sublime before it was eventually altered until it is now unrecognisable in its present state.

We see that time and man has altered this into a myriad of varying beliefs within the title of Buddhism.

For the purpose of this book I shall try to place as many of the similar beliefs together as possible.

There are, Buddha says, several truths:-
Firstly that we are all born for trouble.
Secondly the cause of unhappiness is the pursuit of pleasure.
Thirdly that we must break free of our physical desires in order to attain the freedom of our soul.

In some aspects of Buddhism there is the eightfold path to enlightenment which some seem to follow as if it were law and some tend to almost ignore. It is as follows:-

Right beliefs
Right ideals
Right speech
Right efforts
Right actions
Right living
Right thoughts
Right meditation

For the Buddha to come up with this path it took the "Immortal One" to enter his soul. I will now set you a task. Go and get a pen, a piece of paper and give yourself ten minutes. Now write down eight ways to a better life. No, not winning the lottery, pretend you are setting up a religion, imagine you're a nun or monk.

Quite simply and without trying to sound too condescending, how many of us, given a pen, a piece of paper and ten minutes would come up with similar ideas? I have tried it on a wide range of people, from Christian to Atheist and found that at least five of the eight are normally written down. A Christian would replace meditation with prayer, but apart from that they sound fairly straightforward. The words of Buddha are not difficult to imagine as being the words of man and are thus not substantial enough to act as proof for god.

Buddha was living in a spiritually buzzing and confused land; people beat themselves to achieve greater spirituality and fasted for years on end. Gautama saw need and tried to fill the gap, a gap which many have tried to fill over the years.

In all my research on Buddhism what keeps coming home is the openness to myth, legend and interpretation. There are so many different kinds of Buddhists that to label them all Buddhists is now all most a farce. It is like naming the cults of the Mormon and Moony as Christians, alongside Catholics and Protestants, but we don't. A Christian is a believer in the Nicene creed which states that Jesus Christ is the Son of god, born of a virgin and crucified on a cross etc. Whereas Mormons also believe in the book written by Joseph Smith and standard Christians do not.

However, Buddhism seems from the outside to be able to skirt such creeds and flow along, as the individual requires. In a way we have to admire this free spirit, but what about truth? It is true that an apple is green, but it can also be red. Indeed on the inside it is white. Surely god is not like this sort of truth. God should be one kind of god only, if he exists outside of us. Should god really be what we want him to be? As the famous Highlander film once said "there can be only one."

Some Buddhists deny the existence of a god, some do not. Some believe in salvation through works, others by faith. They have a mixed bag called Heterodox, which is a sublime mix of ideas such as materialism and Jainism (asceticism). Buddhism is apparently the middle way. There are two main Buddhist traditions. Mahayana and Hinayana, or liberal and conservative beliefs. As for the scriptures of Buddhism, which would have been, useful tools on checking out which of the many Buddhists were right, we find that none of them can be trusted. In this Buddhism does not differ at all from any of the other religions. The scriptures were blatantly adapted and changed without apology. It seems that Buddhist monks were not quite as scholarly in preserving their scriptures as were the Jews.

Now we must turn to the Buddhist ideology of rebirth. There are problems here. It is the Buddhist idea that we are on a continual cycle of life, death and rebirth. Each turn of the cycle we are meant to improve ourselves and eventually achieve release from the cycle. However, we have to ask ourselves the following questions. Why do we not remember our past lives? What happens when the sun finally burns up and life on earth is no more? Where do we go then? There are supposedly six realms after ours, where are they and why have we not yet found them whilst exploring the local parts of our galaxy? We could very well be eating our Grandmothers every time we bite into a Big Mac as Buddhism allows for rebirth as animals. Indeed, somebody may very well eat you in your next life, especially if you have not been good enough in this life.

The Dalai Lama claims that the meaning of life is as follows:-

If all these rebirths keep happening and everybody's Karma keeps getting better and better then eventually the world will be perfect.

There is an unfortunate problem here. Things are not getting better. We still have wars, terrorists still hurtle planes into populated buildings, nuclear war and accidents are still not a thing of the past, forest fires, earthquakes, murders, rape, disease child abuse and much more are still very much a part of our lives. History is a cycle, it repeats itself and we never learn from it. There are simply too many years of evolutionary constraints upon our minds to stop us fighting each other. The world is still a volatile place, even after millions of supposedly Karma improving rebirths.

Whichever way we look at it, Buddhism, through Mahayana, Hinayana, Zen or Tao, we come across problems. There is a lack of historical data. There is no scientific basis for rebirth and scriptural evidence is patchy. There are contradictions just like any other religion and to top all of that the orange robes would clash awfully with my hair.

When a young man called Sariputta said to the Buddha, "Lord, such faith have I in the exalted one that methinks there never has been, nor will be, nor is there now any other who is greater and wiser than the exalted one." He was contradicted by the Buddha who replied that to make such statements one must know all Buddha's past, present and future. Here we have an insight. That Buddha knew he was not the only "special" person in the world or indeed history. That there had been spiritual leaders in the past, in the present and that there would be in the future. The future was wide open to new possibilities. Maybe we should take this Buddha at his words and keep a look out for the next one. Then again maybe Buddha, as outlined in The Shining Ones (radikalbooks.com) was really a main player in a worldwide conspiracy of deceit and control.

Is Allah the Answer?

Islam is one of today's strongest and most powerful religion's, with one in seven people, or 500 million devout Muslims and growing by the day. The word Islam means literally to surrender and thus a Muslim is the name given to those who submit in surrender to Allah.

From thousands of Minarets the words "god is most great" cry out as the Muezzin or crier calls the people to prayer. In droves they come to prostrate themselves towards Muhrab or the wall that faces Mecca. The great Imans, Ayatollahs or Mullahs hold sway over millions of people worldwide and guide mighty armies of believers in whatever course Allah decides.

But why? Where did all this originate? And from whom?

The monotheistic religion of Islam springs from the same source stream as Christianity and Judaism and originated in around 571AD when a man called Muhammad was born to a family named Hashem in or around the city of Mecca. According to Dr Bouqet in his book "Comparative Religion" when speaking about Muhammad "there is little known that can be called history".

At this time there was a vacuum of power between the two great imperialistic nations of Persia and Byzantium, leaving the area around Mecca vulnerable to great change. It was a prosperous area, but as Muhammad grew to find out, it was anarchical in its way of life. People worshipped many gods or demigods, and raised great monoliths in order to appease these wild human-like deities.

Against this background little Muhammad was raised. His parents had died whilst he

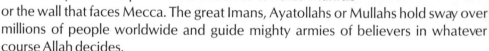

was still young and he appears to have been passed around the remaining family until eventually he ended up with his uncle, Abu Talib. Whilst under his care, Muhammad was employed in the family firm and travelled up and down the country and into Syria with the camel trains. Of course this lead to him receiving all kinds of early influences from Arabs, Jews and Christians, and probably being totally confused as to which one was right. Although there is evidence that he saw Christianity as a rather corrupt guise of the true religion. Imagine then, seeing your own kind worshipping a bewildering variety of gods and then these foreigners worshipping their gods also, in your land.

Muhammad was a strong willed young man by all accounts and like you or I, had ideals. He seems to have had respect for the Jews and Christians but wanted to find some way of bringing the faiths together under one powerful new religion, that was acceptable to the Arabs. At least that is the official line of the Islamic historians. It may very well be that Muhammad was purely the pawn of a much greater and more ancient plan of power control which is outlined in my other book The Shining Ones (radikalbooks.com).

During all this, Muhammad, now a man of 25 was proposed to by a 40 year old woman called Khadija. He accepted and they were married, having six children, one of them being Fatima (meaning The Shining One).

He became a hanif: a kind of wandering ascetic and he began a growing fear of demons, hearing voices in his head. Of course we only have the Islamic history textbooks to prove this and it seems there can be only a couple of rational explanations. He was going mad, there really were demons talking to him in his head which is scientifically impossible or this is the addition of a later scholar to make Muhammad seem more plausible as a spiritual leader, rather than a warrior leader which he surely was. I plump for the latter.

The rest of the story of Muhammad is simply a collection of traditions, which are equally as unbelievable. It seems that after retreating to a cave one day he was called upon by the angel Gabriel (a Jewish and Christian character also used by the secret societies of the Jews as a messenger to install the next line of leader). Gabriel revealed to Muhammad a scroll of flaming words. Now, even though Muhammad could not read, he read this. Please note at this juncture that there were no witnesses, much like Joseph Smith finding his tablets of god. So we are left with 500 million people living according to the words of a man (or group of men) who claim that Gabriel revealed flaming words in a cave. We only have the words of Muhammad. Not admissible as evidence I am afraid.

Admittedly when Muhammad told people this he was persecuted, that is, according to the texts we have. Eventually however people came around and started to believe this strange man. At first it was just his wife, but then came the slaves of Mecca, who, not surprisingly, wanted to follow this powerful orator who promised freedom.

In due course Muhammad upset too many people and found himself ostracised from Mecca and moved with his converts to Medina. Here the Jews rejected him as a heretic, but ultimately he gained support amongst the more dejected Arabs.

Problems arose for various reasons and a small battle ensued between his followers and the merchants of Mecca. Muhammad was victorious and in the eyes of the Arabs that could only mean one thing: god was on his side.

At the age of 60 he took an army and marched upon his designated holy city of Mecca. He took it without mercy, his followers killing man, woman and child. Two years later he died. Now the converts of Islam had a prime example to follow.

Before he died however, this great religious leader supposedly wrote the Koran (Qu'ran, meaning that which is uttered) which in part, is a collection of fragments of other beliefs. Muhammad reportedly went into a seizure prior to reciting the book. This book in turn was then copied with true fundamentalist fervour and is, according to Islamic scholars, as good a record of the original as possible. Of course, for the most part, having been copied from other beliefs and altered to suit, many of the stories are in parallel to the Old Testament. Such as Abraham having two wives, one named Sarah and one called Haggai. The Koran tells us that Haggai having given birth to Abraham's child was sent off into the wilderness where her offspring became the forefathers of the Arabs.

In fact, much interbreeding still occurred in Muhammad's day between Jews and Arabs and thus traditions were easily passed on, such as Old Testament stories. It is plainly obvious upon reading the Koran and the Old Testament that they are intrinsically linked together both in content and spiritual ideology.

The Koran account of Jesus is claimed to be the true story of this enigmatic individual and although the Bible is believed to be a god-given and god-inspired book, Muslims believe it is only second best and that the Koran is the latest revelation of a most high god. Indeed, they claim that the Bible had been altered much. A claim, which has stood the test of time, especially when we understand that people in the west would not have realised that the text of the Bible had in fact been altered much. Muhammad was in the prime location to utilise this information to enable his own power base to be built.

In the section of the Koran called Sura 19:92 it states, "Jesus Christ, the son of Mary, was no more than an Apostle of god." This obviously contradicts the New Testament, which states Jesus to be much more, at least by the Pauline creed.

Muslims also say that Christ was not crucified, but that somebody took his place. Almost 1500 years before the internet these Muslims seem to have developed their own idea of a conspiracy theory, coming remarkably close to the truth and giving us an insight into what really occurred at "Golgotha".

Of course, it may be that this was just Muhammad's attempt at bringing the religions of the world together. However these ideas were not original and probably not even his. Gnostic's had been following a similar belief for many years, spreading their apocryphal word across the length and breadth of Arabia.

Being fair to Islam, we certainly can see the strength of belief and conviction inherent within the structure of this system. There may be many things wrong with Islam, I am not an Islamic scholar, but there are a lot of satisfied people within Islam. The very fact that Muslims are so fundamental in their beliefs, devout in their worship and patient in carrying out their creeds is commendable. It shows, at least, the deep held belief of 500 million people that there is a god and although this is not Proof of god's existence it is strong circumstantial evidence.

Could it be that there is an empty space or vacuum, inside each one of us that just cries out for god and knows that he exists in one form or another? But is this evidence for god? No. It just shows that we, as the highest level of life on earth, even now, in today's age, still need a god of some kind. It may be some kind of evolutionary survival trick which our minds play on us. If it is then it has been playing that game for a very long time. From the early beginnings, from the beliefs in solar and lunar deities, anthropomorphic figures of power have held our imaginations. Religion, like us and with us has evolved.

Had we still held to our belief in a lunar deity then we would now have our answer as to whether there was a god or not. But the evolution of religion and belief remained one step ahead of us and when we finally set foot on the grey dust of our ladies surface we found that she was nothing more than an old spherical pile of rubble. Of course we already knew.

In conclusion and for the purposes of this book we can see that millions of people believe in something and that they believe they see a wonderful order and course to our lives, even amidst such obvious turmoil. It is not surprising when we consider the numerous other defence mechanisms our physical body utilises to defend us from invading armies of bacteria that our mental body defends us against the invading doubts and worries of a fragile life.

We still however have no proof one way or the other for god.

The Case For Christ

Christianity is one of the world's largest religions. Within the title fall many denominations such as Catholicism and Anglicanism and most (but by no means all) follow the Nicene Creed. However, we are not, in the context of this book interested in the various splits and separations which have occurred over the past two thousands years, unless they hold some kind of evidence for or against the existence of god. The majority of the splits have been created by the dogmas, doctrines and power hungry acts of man. We are interested in what Christianity has to say about god.

Christians say quite simply that they are born again of the Spirit of god and believe in Jesus Christ as their saviour and creator. A tall order for any man.

We have stories from the Bible about Jesus, which we will draw strongly upon. The reason for this being quite simply that there is precious little said about Jesus in other texts and that it is the Bible that is utilised by Christians to prove his existence. There are stories of his birth and life, which we should all be familiar with by now and none of which can be proven.

He is known by many names and each name explains a different aspect of the belief of Christians. This is partly due to the Hebrew language, which has many more levels than our simple English in comparison and partly due to the fact that we are talking about an amalgamation of religious ideas.

The name Jesus means saviour and when used in conjunction with Christ, which means anointed one we simply have "anointed saviour". In Hebrew the term messiah also means anointed one. To be anointed means to be god's chosen one. One thing that Christians forget to tell us is that there were many chosen one's and messiahs spilling in and around the Middle East at this time, and indeed for hundreds of years. Jesus was almost a common name and he would have had to have been something special to have made his mark. As we saw even Buddha said that there were many before and many after, a true understanding of the nature of mankind.

Another phrase in Matthew 16:16 is "Immanuel". This means "god with us", which could have immense scope and meaning in itself. It is taken from Amun-U-el, an Egyptian phrase also meaning the Shining One is with us (see The Shining Ones radikalbooks.com).

The manhood and Godhead of Jesus is shown also in the label "Son of god", which supposedly reveals the distinctive relationship between god as father and god as son. Indeed anyone who makes such a claim must either be mad, telling the truth or have some kind of hidden agenda. The truth? Judaism preached that all Jews were indeed the Sons of god and this title was nothing more than a description of membership to the guild of Judaism. Jesus was no lunatic, but neither was he any more the son of god than you or I. Indeed he even went as far as he could to bring this ideology home to the masses, only to be hijacked later by Pauline doctrine overlaying the message with stronger methods of power control.

Many diverse titles give us yet more insights to this enigmatic character. Son of David manifests the role of the coming messiah which Jews believed strongly should have been a warrior king and in the line of David. There is evidence to show that Jesus was indeed a warrior king, with even scriptural evidence of his disciples carrying swords, and indeed using them.

The Servant description is the fulfilment of the Jehovah servant role, which had been prophesied in the Old Testament, and anybody interested in writing up the account of Jesus would have been obliged to include this description in his biography.

The very fact that Jesus came, in order to bear our transgressions, instead of the usual sacrificial lamb offering of the Jews at the time, explains the identity Lamb of God. In becoming the offering himself, Jesus is said to take away the need for a mediator and priest, becoming the High Priest himself on our behalf. Ultimately Jesus falls in this sacrifice and is called the Last Adam, the righter of the wrong.

Thus in the very names applied to him, we see the fulfilment of much so called prophecy and much need. The prophecy of the Jews however is like any other, changeable with the times and perfectly self-fulfilling.

According to the legend Jesus was rejected by the people he came to serve. Did he know that he would be rejected? Is that the idea? That only those with real faith would believe in him? Theologically it could make sense or it could simply be that even the people from his period did not believe in him and therefore why should we?

So, lets now have a look at what he did to receive these names. We all know those now famous nativity scenes. The manger with a few lambs, a goat, a window through which we can see a shooting star, Mary and Joseph stood adoringly above the cot within which lies the baby Jesus. However, looking into the actual writings from the period and forgetting all the man made marketing nonsense of the past hundred years we suddenly find that our memories are filled with a false record. Which in itself is not a major problem, it just means that the very first encounter with Jesus turns out to be nothing more real than Santa Claus. There are many reasons for the symbolisms within the myth, none of which goes any way towards proving the existence of god.

From the Bible we learn that the Magi see the new baby as an illustration that the existing mystical hierarchy of religion rejoiced in the Lord's coming. Of course, we must remember that much of this was written many years after the death of Jesus.

Jesus escaped the threat of Herod and ran to Egypt with his parents. There it is believed Jesus learned from the Essene group known as the Theraputae. The great knowledge of Egypt was a draw to many mystics and centres of learning were set up everywhere. These Theraputae were especially skilled in healing, a remarkable and miraculous gift identified in Jesus later in his life. It is without doubt that Jesus must have learned this skill here in Egypt. A remarkable revelation, which pours cold water on the idea that Jesus, had miraculous healing powers from god. We also learn that both Joseph, the father of Jesus and Zechariah the father of John the Baptist, were members of the Theraputae.

Next we find Jesus ready for his appointed ministry, missing many years of his life in-between. Many years spent learning the healing ministry, scriptures and leadership qualities. Jesus was baptised by the one called John in the River Jordan, again self fulfilling as much prophecy as possible. The powers of healing showed by Jesus at this time were so great that even the occupying Romans were said to have begged him to cure their sick.

Slowly now, towards the end of the great play he moved towards Jerusalem, apparently knowing what the outcome was to be. This is plainly evident in his words to his disciples. It proved to be bitterly true as the Pharisee joined with the Sadducee and Herodian in a terrible plot that would inevitably fulfil the greatest of prophecies. I must say that I have a totally different opinion to the normal view of this part of the life of Jesus. I believe that Jesus was part of the plot and a conspirator himself in a much larger plan of control, with a long and far-reaching global ideology. However I must confine myself to the remit of this book, which is evidence for the existence of god, and leave you to read The Shining Ones if you are interested in finding out the truth behind the plot of the passion play.

So what is said about the character of this founder of faith? Above all he had integrity, a trait much admired by many that wrote of him. He had courage, strength and compassion for mankind. Buddhist's say that Christ was enlightened - a great compliment. The Muslims and Jews say that he was surely a great prophet. Even the great cults of our age misuse his name because of the idea of what he was.

What about the cultures of the day? Here, we find that Romans were occupiers of the Jewish nation and thus held them under oppression. They were taxed heavily and their own spiritual leaders, it seems, had sold out. There erupted various sects within Judaism such as the Zealots and the Essenes who were partially violent and erratic. Although they were also adapting and moving with the times. There is much evidence that once their plans were complete they simply disbanded, changed names and became something else.

We should also remember the origins of the literalist view of Jehovah. This vague fertility god was instigated as the Jewish and Christian god by literalists as an answer to the idea of one god. In truth, attributes of many gods were included into the remit of Jehovah. Ra, Horus, El and many other Middle Eastern gods were chosen and their ideologies incorporated for popular success. This is why the god has so many names in the Bible, and many, almost Egyptian deity traits. But we lose sight of the fact that Jehovah was a vengeance god. In the first book of Samuel he takes vengeance on the men of Gath and gives them all haemorrhoids. In Deuteronomy the Israelites are ordered to destroy the people of cities that he bestows upon them. Men are ordered to be stoned to death, plagues are sent, first born children massacred, human sacrifice, and we are even to have no contact with menstruating females. Not to mention that we can buy slaves, give the death sentence to people who work on the Sabbath and that eating shellfish is an abomination. It is therefore no surprise that we expect god to supply us with a vengeful and warrior like messiah.

God had indeed been promising the people a messiah. Or to look at it another way, the people writing the prophecies had been keeping the people happy and looking forward to the saving graces of a warrior leader. This was applied on many levels, both through the auspices of standard religion and as an undercurrent of rebellion. However it was put across, the people wanted it. He was going to unite the various sects and lead them to a glorious victory. Much like the revolutionary figure of Muhammad six hundred years later. It seems that the people never expected a peaceful man, and indeed there is a growing amount of evidence to prove that Jesus was not a peaceful man and could very well have been the warrior King that the people had been waiting for.

Whatever is believed about Christ, we are told not to think of him as the victim of a cruel plot, but rather the victorious leader in all events. This is biblically evident in all he supposedly said and did. It is beyond doubt that Christ was to hand over his life as the definitive sacrifice, this, after all, had been prophesied, and we all know by now that if it is prophesied it just has to come true, even if it is made to happen.

However much we argue the minor elements of the passion play though we cannot argue with the final tenet. That Christianity states simply that it is purely by believing in Jesus Christ as saviour that we are fulfilled. This is the only way of truly knowing that god exists.

We can prove or disprove, relative to whom wishes to believe, that god exists or not simply by mathematics and causal effects, but why should this prove Jesus? Well it doesn't. But surely, as the argument goes, if we can prove the scriptures through history, science and mathematics then we are also proving that Jesus existed as it states in the Bible. Other secular writers did speak of a Jesus; they did show that what had occurred was indeed significant. We are still uncovering evidence about the life of the real Jesus (if indeed there was even such a man) and we may yet prove that there was something very special about the man. After all, he has changed the face of the world and he still changes people, even in death. But there are a few problems.

1)   Jesus was just a good man.

The Christian answer to this one is that firstly he not only taught how to live; he supposedly lived it himself. He called us to lay down our lives for our sisters and brothers and did so himself in the greatest sacrifice, whether a true death or mock sacrifice. He forgave people their sins, something according to Jewish Law at that time and still today is the sole role of god. He claimed to be the truth, life and the way of god. He allowed people to worship him as if he were god, was this delusion of grandeur or simply excellent propaganda. Either he was deranged, very clever or he was god. Everything he did and said was calm and calculated, especially when compared to some of the worlds other religious leaders. But what if Christ was in it for the glory and the fame? Any psychological study of the mind of Jesus will and has shown a stable, truthful man. But all this could simply be the result of good writing; there is no proof either way.

2)   Christ's virgin birth.

The people in the time of Christ were just as sceptical of this as many are today. The people thought Mary had been unfaithful to Joseph and indeed so did Joseph for a time. They knew too then, that virgin births were just not possible. Yet we have many people writing about it alongside perfectly ordinary facts. We cannot believe one without the other, if one is proved correct the other must also be. Either that, or there must be another reason for this strange entry into the world.

According to Christians Jesus was not an ordinary person. He was the Son of God and perfect. He had already pre-existed in the beginning as the Word. Through this word all things were made, it is not then a far leap for this Word to become flesh. If we cannot believe in the Virgin birth then we cannot believe in the creation and we are left with a Universe that only theoretically exists. Only by granting god the power of creation can we grant him the power to intercede in such a way. If it is true then we should say Mary is blessed, as she had that power of god within her when he altered DNA and became flesh.

However there is another explanation. There was at the time of Christ a cult within the Jewish faith called "the cult of the virgin". This was a female sect, well respected and well known at the time.

The basic precepts of the cult were also well known and worldwide. For instance Isis immaculately conceived Horus in Egyptian mythology.

Virgil had said that the Messiah would be born of a virgin, Zoroaster was born of a virgin and later Muhammad's daughter Fatima (meaning shining one) gave birth to 3 sons and was said to be a virgin.

It seems then that the virgin ideal, was a predominant idea for any messenger or messiah of god. There could easily be another plan in play here, a plan which has no bearing on proof for god, however this is taken up in my other book "The shining ones".

3)   Why is this Jesus relevant? The Christian response.

Firstly, although it is a little used word in this modern age, the Bible says all have sinned and fall short of the glory of god. Is there anybody out there who thinks they are better or equal to god? How can we cope with all our imperfections, meet a god of holiness and expect mercy? Can you imagine the holiness of the god who created everything? We cannot meet god by ourselves, in that sinful state, so therefore we need help or saving. So therefore, apparently, Jesus is our saviour?

Secondly, he is an example to us, the way we ought to be. If only we all turned the other cheek and loved our neighbours as ourselves. If only we loved, even unto death. The way of Christ is the way of god. Jesus is relevant if I want to alter the world and make it a better place to live, that is of course if I believe in god? But it must be belief, which is faith not proof.

4)   Why is there evil in the world?

Firstly I would like to throw one question back at you. If god were to wipe out all the evil in the world today, right now, at this moment in time, where would that leave you? It would leave the world without human beings, for where does this evil manifest itself unless it is in us?

Secondly, let us then agree that there is such a thing on the planet called evil. Now let us agree that we do not need gods help to stop it, after all we are doing a good job now are we not?

Who then shall we turn to? The gods of our television screen? Mad Max or Rambo? Or maybe plump for the old crystals to calm ourselves down and smoke an illegal substance for relaxation?
So what have we replaced god with? Are they not all empty things? Are we not perpetuating evil ourselves?
Now, in this world there seems to be certain things men of standing cannot explain, those inner and almost universal feelings of love for instance, although it is coming to light that there is a hormone responsible.
Why do we sense goodness in ourselves when we have helped another in a needy situation?
Why do we feel guilt when we have refused that person help?
Ever since mans beginning he has rebelled against god. But some say, "Why didn't god create man perfect?" The Christian answer is he did. But he had to give us free will, so that we were not zombies and loved him by ourselves and not because he commanded us to.

It is man who is at fault for the state of the world. That by our sin, by our greed and lust, we allow evil to take over in our lives. This in itself shows that unique link between man and his surroundings. It is us who affect the Earth and all that live upon it, it is us who can make it better. In faith god supposedly gives us the power to do this, for surely in our power alone we cannot, this we have already proved with every life that is lost through war.

According to Christians, god gave us a way out of this vicious cycle of hate and intolerance. We can never understand all that god does for us, but according to Christianity he bore the evil in death and defeated it in his resurrection. He proved that we could succeed with his help. Does this have a ring of truth? Remember you will be asked for a verdict, if not by me, then you're own sub-conscious.

All these reasons have been used now for thousands of years against us. Convincing us that we are not good enough to better the world on our own, that we need to tie ourselves to a religion and follow dogma and doctrine to see a more peaceful existence. This could all so very easily be put down as good propaganda, as clever usage of the facts to get us to follow. It could just be that we are who we are because of evolution. The simple survival of the fittest, the strongest gains all the power and wealth.

No god here, no amount of humility will help us, apart from make us feel more relaxed with being controlled by those with the power. Giving us good reason to do as we are told.

We still have no hard evidence either way for god's existence.

GETTING CLOSE TO THE TRUTHS

- The great Esoteric Jigsaw Puzzle

From the religions of ages past we can glean certain truths that man in his searching has either come across or been given. These examples remarkably resemble other beliefs, making one wonder, where did they originate ? And why? Whatever the answer is, we can at least see that they stand alone in certain statements and that sometimes other religions get close to the truth. These cross references with ancient belief are claimed by Christians to be proof in themselves that, there must be something more than fanciful imagination.

Could it be that these are echoes from the past? That the word of creation spread around the planet as people migrated? Passing on knowledge by word of mouth in this great, esoteric jigsaw puzzle?

Was there some great and ancient universal religion or priesthood managing our beliefs?

Take for instance the following-

1) The Satapatha Brahmana tells us quite specifically how god spoke everything into existence, the Earth, air, sky and animals. This is fairly similar to the Bible as so far as god spoke creation into existence with the Word. ("And god said ......" Genesis 1:3)

2) The Taittiriya Brahmana tells us again that the entire Universe was created by god and gives account of him breathing life into a child, thus becoming the father. ("..breathed into his nostrils the breath of life." Genesis 2:7)

3) The Satapatha Brahmana says that god made man from his soul, then due to mans loneliness he caused the man to fall into two parts, "Thence arose a husband and wife. From them men were born." ("Then the lord god made a woman from the rib he had taken out of man." Genesis 2:22)

4) According to the Vishnu Purana, Brahma (god) exists as spirit. ("god is spirit.....," John 4:24)

5) In Egyptian mythology Khepera (god) formed the whole world "out of his mouth." He apparently laid first the foundations and then all things, as the sequence of the Bible shows.

6) In Celtic folklore there was primarily just god until he again spoke existence into being. ("And god said.....")

7) In ancient Peru they stated that all things were created by the word of the spirit or creator. Such words as "Let a man be. Let a woman be. " Also, man was made of clay as in the Biblical creation and possibly also a belief many thousands of years old.

8) The south American Indians believe that the material Universe was first created, then man and woman were formed from the clay and split apart, therefore making them separate and able to produce offspring. They still hold to this belief and the immortality of their soul depends upon it.

Notice that the above comparisons are about creation. This is something that all mankind has to have before his religion.
It is not specific to Christianity or Judaism. Each and every person on the planet has the same origins. Therefore the various stories should all lead back to the one basic truth. But is everything truth?

Many religions hold dear the idea of a Ring of truth. That a certain ideal sounds true and therefore must be true. This is used as evidence. But it isn't evidence. Never the less lets take a look at some that simply "sound" unfeasible.

IS THERE SUCH A THING AS A RING OF TRUTH?

There is a bewildering complexity of organisations; establishments and fanatics all geared up with an array of imaginative ideas.

1) Scientologists believe that an alien named Xenu was the leader of the Universe about seventy five million years ago. One day he decided that he needed more dwelling space and nuked Earth, thus creating Thetans or spirits which attach themselves to our bodies making us unclean. Speaking about the creation of all things the holy words of Ron Hubbard (Creator of Scientology, a science fiction

writer) states, "Loud snap. Waves of light. Chariot comes out, blows horn, comes close. Shattering series of snaps, Cherub fades back. Blackness dumped on Thetan." Need I say more?

2) The followers of Krishna have some unusual beliefs as explained by the Divine Grace Bhakdivedanta Swami Prabhupada. Jesus Christ was not god, but a devotee of Krishna visiting from another planet! Men are superior to women. ANY action done for Krishna cannot be bad. Needless to say there are only 15000 followers worldwide and this mainly due to the ex-Beatle George Harrison.

3) Another famous personality who followed a cult is Pete Townsend of the Who, a devotee of Meher Baba. This strange Indian was one of the latest self-professed saviours. Apparently his soul will return to stone from whence it came. Meher Baba died of natural causes surprisingly and is buried.

4) More stars again as we turn to the Osmond's, the teenage idols of the seventies. They were supposedly devout Mormons (The church of Jesus and the Latter Day Saints,) Donny however has revealed sordid tales of his youth.

The book of Mormon was (supposedly) written during, and covers the period between 600 BC and 400 AD, yet surprisingly contains many Bible passages in the exact same translation as that of the Authorised King James Bible of 1611 AD, therefore either the King James Bible is stolen from the book of Mormon (which can be proved to be untrue) or the book of Mormon is stolen from the King James version (which is more likely).

They claimed that the book was error free. Since 1830 AD there have been 3913 changes, most of these changes were the very parts that had been changed from the King James Version. They claimed archaeological evidence existed for their belief that an ancient tribe of Jews lived in America. No such evidence exists and this is attested to by all Americas leading historians.

Between 1809 and 1812 AD a man called Solomon Spalding wrote an imaginary history of two civilisations coming to America (remarkably like the book of Mormon). Solomon died, but the manuscript was left in the printer's office where another man called Sidney Rigdon worked. Later Sidney met Joseph Smith, who later still went on to write the book of Mormon. Joseph Smith and his brother Hyrum were jailed awaiting trial, but on 27th June 1844 two hundred men broke in and shot them both dead.

5) The Hindu's have literally hundreds of god's. They are dressed in pretty clothes, coloured brightly and fed expensive food. They are probably the best-kept dolls on earth. If you are going to believe in a god it may as well be a Barbie doll.

6) Koreshian's believed that everything was within the confines of the earth. That when you look up, you are actually looking inward, towards the sun, which is at the centre of all things.

In 1908 the leader, Dr Cyrus Tweed died 3 days prior to Christmas day. His followers wholeheartedly expected him to rise again on Christmas day. Strangely he failed to do so.

7) The Flat Earth Society is still crusading against the damnable, heretical, globularist conspiracy. In other words, they say that the earth is flat, we never went to the moon, that Arthur C. Clarke scripted the whole thing and the rest of us are mad.

This last exercise is purely and simply to show how witless and lamentable man can be in his exorbitant efforts of searching. The western world has now taken into it's heart the new religions, the television, the Internet, gadgetry, high powered jobs. The rest of the world is too busy trying to kill each other or catch up with us (while we sell them the arms and keep them back through corrosive interest payments). Never the less, eyes are taken off that thing we once called god. And yet, there is still something missing. Evolution has played us a cruel card with this device, this mechanism of self-control. We fill in this gap with our modern day gimmicks, failing to fulfil the real need. Christian's say that this gap only appeared when we walked away from god. They also say that the answer to all our questions came 2000 years ago and we failed to see it.

Atheists on the other hand are just as happy to do their best for mankind, without the need for a god and somehow seem to be just as happy and fulfilled as Christians are. (I know I have over generalised, but the argument would be too long without.)

Conclusion

From the above study then, we can draw certain conclusions. First and foremost is the plain fact that man is searching.

What is he searching for? Fulfilment?

Why would man be searching for fulfilment? Is it because he has an emptiness within that needs to be filled? A subtle awareness of an awesome presence and a need to know his future due to his fears of the unknown? The unfortunate reality is that man first looks to the world for this need and then, when he finds that this cannot fulfil him he then turns to god. It could very well be that neither of these are correct! It may very well be that we should listen to our elders from the past and search inside ourselves for our own fulfilment. As many have said, we are our own gods.

However, man has done a pretty good job so far of distracting himself from the very questions, which burn inside of him.

These questions are answered to varying degrees by all the religions of the world. Our question here is surely, which one is right?

Let us then lay out the questions we need to ask to enable us to choose which, if any, of the religions are correct.

Does the chosen religion sound right? Does it have a ring of truth? Be careful here, a ring of truth is different to many cultures.
Is the religion simple enough for everyone to understand? Surely, if the religion is from a loving god then it needs to be for everybody, both intellectual and simple?
Is the originator of the religion worthy of our praise? How can we judge this? Was he (or she) peaceful? Surely, religious leaders should not be war like? Were they in the business of belief for their own benefit, or those of others? Were they trying to glorify a god, or themselves? What would they gain from their leadership? How far were they prepared to go? Even to death?

If they did go to death, then what for? Did they steal something, kill someone or just speak the truth? Did they basically die for what is right?

Did the death have a reason? Were they totally sane? What influences applied? What hope does the religion give? How can we get it?

Will we have to buy it?

What is the currency?

Hard work? Labour? Money? Or love?

Or is it by the grace of god?

Surely we must not pick on the religion, but the originators. It was they who set the thing in motion and it is to them that we must attribute blame, shame or glory. Each and every religion has been sullied by man's foolishness at one point or another and it is for this reason that we must clear away the mess and get back as close as possible to the originator.

In essence then, we are looking for fulfilment in the very real man of Buddha, Muhammad or Christ. We look to them for our needs, hoping that they will have the answer that we can understand that they will lead us to god.

So just what are our needs?

Everybody needs love. Why? Because quite simply it makes us tick. Love is an evolutionary tool, which drives us as a species and as an individual. Love is one of those bewildering words, which makes you sit down and actually think about your life. It causes pain and joy. Without it we suffer, with it we rejoice. According to most religions, god is love. Therefore, when god is in control, love is in control. A good thing, many of us would agree. However, love can also make us do things we would normally not do, such as invade other countries, kill out of jealousy, be proud and delight in the downfall of those we inevitably end up hating. That is why religious writings talk about a perfect love. One that is painless giving, enduring, never failing, always kind, not proud or self seeking, does not delight in evil and always hopes. Yes, you guessed impossible love.

However, if we were to believe that this kind of love were impossible then we would need help. Lo and behold we have god, who can help us with this love. He can pass us the power of his love via his Holy Spirit.

Surely then, the proof for god, is not in the practical things, like trying to find proof, but maybe the proof has always been in us? In the love that we always have trouble explaining. We recognise our own love for one another, we would die to save our wife or child and according to the religions of the world that's what god would do for us - his children.

Everybody needs security. Why? Because we live in an unsure world. We could be mugged tomorrow or run over by a bus. Our seemingly small, insignificant lives become more than significant when confronted with a lack of security. It is one of those marvellous false ideals that our parents can give us this safety. That they can put their loving arms around us and protect us. There is, according to various religions, at the end of the day, only one father who can protect us properly. Only he can guide us through the turmoil we call life. But this may just be applying a false hope, a false person onto an imaginary problem. Nobody else on earth can fulfil all requirements we have for god and so we create one.

When we are children we make up imaginary friends. Will give them all the various attributes required to be our special friend. We never tell our children to stop doing this, because we know it is good for them and their development. It can give them a sense of security. If they are still talking to shadows at thirty then we must worry and talk seriously about where things have gone wrong. Surely now, mankind has grown up and no longer needs imaginary friends? Or has it?

According to Christian's today, god came to earth in the manifestation of Jesus Christ because we are those little children and he recognised that we could not be left "home alone". That we needed his company again, just like in the Garden of Eden. Even Lord Byron wrote "If ever a man was god or god was man, Jesus Christ was both." Christianity has used the imaginary friend of Jesus Christ ever since and for every occasion. But it also had an added incentive for us to believe that he was the true guide. He was the "son" of god. Muhammad was just another prophet, Buddha just enlightened. Neither was the son of god.

On the simple level that this statement exists then this was a major coup to Christianity. Unfortunately it was a vastly over simplified statement. According to Jewish tradition, we are all sons of god. In fact, at the basic root of all religions, we are all sons of god.

However, here we have found one of the major problems with religion. Over simplification. Necessary oversimplification.

There are so many faiths, so many subtleties with each faith, so many splits in each faith, so much to learn, that we by needs sake, oversimplify. And by allowing ourselves to be caught in this web of deceit we throw away an exciting ride of discovery. Of finding a fantastic world of adventure along the byways of religion. We have one life, why choose one religion? Journey through them all and become a master initiate. Find your own path by walking the many paths of the world. There are without doubt, many thousands of years of truth and mystery tied up in the texts of our world's religions. It can be a very fulfilling trip of discovery to journey with them.

Some say it is through an inner revelation of the truth, a being born again to a new life that is now possible to us, through their own chosen religion. But in the end, this is only possible through a belief system and not through proof. Proof talks to the brain. Belief talks to the heart. When you find belief, you will eventually find faith. If that is what you want.

So, in conclusion. Which god to choose? Which one is real? If any? What price shall we pay for our belief? Shall we have our Thetan's removed by the Scientologists? Shall we remain sceptics, sit on the fence or fall off altogether? Shall we follow the Buddha, the enlightened one? Or are we more inclined towards the very human Muhammad? Maybe, because of our western cultural backgrounds we will follow the way of Christ, and try to forget all that has been done in his name.

The choice is, as always, yours. But you must so far do this, still, without any proof.

Pages of Truth?

A very close relative of mine once said, "You cannot prove anything, religion is a sham."

It is a terrible shame that this is a popular belief. Religion is far from a sham. Nothing so highly organised, on such a vast scale and lasting for such a long time could possibly be called a sham. And yet there is a certain element, which is true. It is sham that religion now fails to address problems today in so many ways. It is a sham that we no longer relate to it, and yet we still need it.

God, has been put on the shelf and forgotten, along with history. We somehow have neglected the ability to learn from either. As the historian, Derek Heater said, "To many of the modern generation, history, like god, is dead."

But, just for argument sake, lets take them both back down off the shelf for this next section and see if we can somehow resolve some historical arguments. Like why is the Bible relevant to us today?

So why is it relevant? Why not forget the Bible and go along with the new religions the world will undoubtedly throw at us in the next few years?

According to Christians it is because it tells us the truth, it tells us about god and it tells us about us.

Frank Morrison attempted to write a book condemning the resurrection as a fallacy. However he had to change his mind. It seems he found so much evidence in favour of an actual supernatural resurrection that he became a Christian and wrote the best selling book "Who moved the stone?"

The very same thing applies to numerous authors, lawyers, scientists, mathematicians, doctors and professional men and women alike. Indeed, I was so surprised upon reading the Lancet (medical professional magazine) at just how strong the debate was still that I was quite disturbed. Does this prove then that we have committed intellectual Christians? And does this prove that there must be a god?

No. There are just as many atheist professionals with just as strong views. Indeed, there are now many hundreds of extremely plausible answers to Frank Morrison's question about who moved the stone. Unfortunately Frank Morrison did not have the Nag Hammadi texts (Dead Sea Scrolls) fully deciphered to help him in his research like many have today. There is a superb (if I do say so myself) theory projected in my book The Shining Ones, regarding the resurrection.

So, let's have a look at some of the well-known historical evidence (so called) for the Bible, which Christians throw down as their gauntlet of evidence.

Jonah

When Jesus walked the planet, the scriptures concerning Jonah were not doubted. In fact Jesus himself spoke of him as if he were an actual character from history (Matthew 12:40). Quite a statement! Let's just take it apart. Jonas is in actual fact Oannes, the Merman and god of Nineveh. Identified with Hea one of the Babylonian trinity and was symbolised as a serpent. Hence Oannes/Jonas being swallowed by a large serpent (Just as Osiris and many other gods of the ancients were). Oannes was a god and a man (probably a prophet), like Jesus; he was also a craftsman, of woodworking. In actual fact, what the words attributed to Jesus were really saying is quite simple. That he would be greater than a serpent god of the Babylonians, or even of a prophet of this god.

Christians also hold up 2 Kings 14:24 as if this backs up the Christian ideas. However this is just a line about the prophet/god called Jonas.

It must be remembered that we have a "giant" problem with names in the Bible, and other old texts. To put it simply, many titles and names are not as they seem. Real men of old lost their actual identities through manipulation of their real lives into the old mystery plays and traditional pagan religions. Jonas literally took on some of the "mysterious" elements of Oannes. Just as Jesus takes on many other characteristics which make him more "believable". Many times these men of renown become giants, and via pagan hating Judaism and Christianity become slow and dumb.

This is also a Gnostic initiation tale. Where there are subtleties of the story of ourselves coming into play. The elements of our own personal subconscious and conscious coming into understanding of who we are. It is a standard method of hiding the truth where only those with the eyes to see will be able to see it. It is the mystery of the understanding of ourselves which is truly at stake here.

The Whale

The animal itself need not have been a whale. This is a mistranslation as the Bible actually calls it a large fish, or serpent. This fish swallowed Jonah and hung on to him for three days and three nights.

So is there or has there ever been a fish or whale which could swallow a man the then spew him out three days later?

The answer is yes. The anatomies of several species are sufficient for the production of oxygen suitable for breathing. Four just such species are the whale shark, the sperm whale, the white shark and the cachalot whale.

In fact this is known to have happened to several seamen of history. The best known and most often quoted by Christian apologetics is the case of James Bartley. Indeed Bartley told his own tale of how when he had been a member of the whaling ship Star of the East, he had fallen overboard. After a day and a half the whale they had been chasing was hauled onto the ship and cut open. Out fell James Bartley. His skin was pure white, having been parched by the gastric juices of the whale's stomach.

Apparently the very same species of whale is known to have swallowed sharks whole and to have vomited them onto the shore later, just as Jonah/Jonas is said to have been spewed ashore.

It is not a stretch of the imagination then for this to have actually happened. However it is part of popular mythology and Shaman magic lore for a prophet or magic man to enter a dark place, cave or womb like structure (such as a pyramid) and remain there for 3 days, prior to being resurrected. Indeed it is part of Judaic mythology as we see with the myth of Lazarus.

Nineveh

Strangely, in the very place Jonas/Jonah ended up, archaeologists found a bas-relief on a wall of a man sticking out of the mouth of a large serpent like fish. This relief is dated to around 800 BC, the very period some say Jonah lived.

Could it be that this very miracle so impressed the people of Nineveh that they erected relief's in his honour? In actual fact, this bas-relief is evidence for the Oannes mythology and cult worship. The two are inextricably linked.

The very same Nineveh was however, once said to be a fable. Yet it was found west of Baghdad. If the city exists, a species capable of fulfilling the scripture exists and the local lore of this man in the mouth of a fish exists, then could it be that there is some truth behind the myth? What more do we need? Unfortunately, faith. The factual evidence of the Bible is not doubted. It is just the interpretation of those facts which is.

The city of Nineveh was said in the Bible to be three days journey across. This is about sixty miles, or twenty miles per day. Dr Layard excavated the ruins of Nineveh. He found that the city was indeed 60 miles in diameter, or 3 days journey. This kind of fact is verifiable and hard. When the Bible says that the Lord spoke, then we do not have verifiable evidence and we have to take faith or dismiss it as being the word of god's chosen elect - priest. In this instance then we can verify that there were priests and we know that they did indeed issue declarations as the word of god.

Famine

In Acts 11:28 there is a prediction that in the reign of Claudius there would be a famine. In the Pembroke collection we find a coin from the era with Claudius on one side and the well-known symbol of famine on the other, a pair of scales and a bushel. Now after archaeological backup we can say that Acts 11:28 was correct. It does not however mean that the prophecy came true, as the book was written after the event.

Paulus

In Acts 13:7 we find that Sergius Paulus was proconsul of Cyprus. However, many historians claimed this to be untrue. But Sir William Ramsay found a stone from the period with the Latin inscription "To Lucius Sergius Paulus the younger, son of

Lucius, one of our commissioners in charge of the Roman Streets, tribune of the soldiers of the sixth legion." He did exist. Also found in Cyprus was a coin from the period stating "In the proconsulship of Paulus." He was a proconsul of Cyprus.

This is therefore proof, from text and archaeology that Luke was strictly correct in his historical writings. But does this mean that everything was correct?

Many years ago I wrote a novel called The Awakening of Manach Mor. It never came to the publisher's desk. However in-order to make the main theme of this surreal fantasy more believable I included many facts. I was only 15 at the time. If I understand the need to include fact to make the fiction more believable, at the tender age of 15, then surely the accumulated intellect of these elders of the church certainly did.

Jupiter and Mercury

Yet again Sir Ramsay found evidence which backed up the writings of Luke. In Acts 14:11,12 Luke wrote about the worship of the gods Jupiter and Mercury at Lycaonia. Many said at the time that this combination of gods was unrealistic and wrong. However a statute dedicated by the Lycaonians was found which blatantly showed both gods in a local cult. Luke was right.

Belshazzar

Many have said that the King of Babylon, Belshazzar, did not exist because he did not appear in any known sources other than the Bible. This was in fact paraded as proof that the Bible did get things wrong. And yet, in a clay cylinder from a Babylonian Temple we find the statement, "In the heart of Belshazzar, my first born son..." And then again in the Sons of Egibi contracts there is a letter to the secretary of Belshazzar. Well done Bible.

Tower of Babel

The Tower of Babel was said to be a myth by many scholars. However a series of cylinders were found at Borshippa which spoke of a tower which was ancient in the days of Nebuchadnezzar. This may mean the Tower of Babel due to the size and evidence of the burnt bricks and bitumen that had been used as mortar. In the British Museum we find a doorstep which had been acquired from the Birs Nimrod Temple commemorating the restoration of the Tower of Babel.

Of course many believe the Tower of Babel to be symbolic of our yearning and striving for god, but either way the Bible is not damaged as theoretically factual.

Attack

A black obelisk, which is in the British Museum, gives us information regarding a story in Kings 10:29-32 regarding the defeat of King Jehu by King Hazeal. Archaeological back up again.

Giants

In Genesis 6:4 we find a rather peculiar statement regarding the existence of giants. Of course we are much too advanced to believe in such things. Or are we? Many Christians believe in the literal truth of these stories and go to any extreme to prove their case. They point out that in folklore around the globe there are many stories of giants, and that many times folklore has been proven to have itself some element of truth deep with in well of mystery. Indeed the EU (European Union) has had to raise doorways internationally to accommodate our growing stature. Could it be that somewhere in our past giants once roamed the land?

Goliath was said to have been about 12 feet in height. The bed of King Og, King of Bashen, is said to have been 18 feet long. In Bashen archaeologists have discovered a massive city where virtually everything is approximately double size, including graves, doorways and stone beds.

However, as stated previously the use of giant language is often to depict the days of old, when things were greater and the rulers are imbued with a giant stature. Many time's real people became gods over time. Look at the myths of Atlantis, Lemuria and King Arthur, where the rulers are taller, stronger and quick-witted.

Stables

In excavations at Tell el-Mutesellim archaeologists found the actual palace, stables and chariot sheds of the governor Baana. This man is spoken of in 1 Kings 14:12. In Megiddo there has been found the massive stables of King Solomon as mentioned in 1 Kings 9:15.

Manna

Who believes in Manna bread said to have been the staple diet of the Israelites whilst wondering in the wilderness? Did god really provide for his people?

Well, the plant called Tamarisk has a strange occupier called Najacocci. This is plant louse, which is white in colour and looks like cotton wool buds. It does not just stay with the Tamarisk however but rests also on grass and stones. In the Middle East this is still eaten as a delicacy and is still available today as Mannite. So whether it was god or not, we shall never know, but nature could certainly have provided. Of course, Manna may also be related to the drug Soma used by Shaman and possibly taken fro snake poison.

Sodom and Gomorrah

Geologists have discovered that around 2000 BC the vale of Sodom plunged into an abyss. At about the same period, according to biblical scholars, Sodom and Gomorrah were destroyed. These two cities were situated in the vale of Sidom.

Further, a Phoenician historian wrote, "The Vale of Sidom sank and became a lake, always steaming and containing no fish, symbol of vengeance and of death for the transgressor."

In Genesis we find the tale of these two cities as they are destroyed because of the transgressions of the inhabitants. People were warned to flee, those who did not were turned to pillars of salt.

Now in the very same area we find the surrounding landscape has volcanoes, layers of basalt and a Dead Sea without fish and so much salt content that we can float in the water. We only have to look at Pompeii to realise that this event in the vale of Sidom was not unrivalled. There are also tablets from the period mentioning Sodom and Gomorrah which were found at Tell Mardikh. The Bible seemingly has the facts and cleverly adapts the obviously terrible circumstances of a natural catastrophe into a lesson for us all - do as god says (or at least the priests who are his mouthpiece).

Jesus

There have been some that have doubted the existence of Jesus and many Christian apologetics have fervently fought the crusade against such blasphemy.

They claim: -

The New Testament contains twenty-seven separate documents written before the end of the first century about Jesus. Nobody in ancient history has the amount of contemporary evidence for his or her existence as Jesus. Whether or not these documents are reliable is another thing, which we will come to shortly.

Flavius Josephus wrote, "Now there was about this time, Jesus, a wise man, for he was a doer of wonderful works - a teacher of such men as receive truth with pleasure."

In Annals, he explains the meaning of the name Christian, "Christ, from whom they derive their name, was condemned to death by the procurator Pontius Pilate."

Suetonius in his book The Twelve Caesars says "He drove the Jews out of Rome who were rioting because of Chrestus." Of course from the 1st century to the 5th we have people who called themselves Chrestians, rather than Christians. The Marcionites claimed to follow Jesus Chrestios (Jesus the Good) rather than Jesus Christus (Jesus the Messiah). Not good evidence therefore for the belief in Jesus as the Messiah, but rather, just as a good man. There is also evidence to suggest that god was proclaimed to be Oannes rather than Yahweh (see Jesus and The Goddess by Timothy Freke and Peter Gandy).

Orosius tells us of the Jews being driven out of Rome also. Indeed Acts 18:2 confirms such events, "Claudius had ordered all the Jews to leave Rome."

Cornelius Tacitus who was a Roman historian wrote of Jesus and the existence of the Christians.

But, are the writings of the New Testament reliable?

Would we say the same thing about Plato? Julius Caesar? Shakespeare? No. And yet, historians essentially believe that these ancient records were written by those named as authors. Yet it is unlikely that these people actually spoke or wrote the words attributed to them. Just as it is unlikely that Jesus spoke any of the words attributed to him.

The problem is that for many hundreds of years the Christian church has manipulated the history and textual evidence to suit its needs. So much so that none of the really crucial elements are now trustworthy. It was indeed, part of the instructions to ensure that all texts followed current dogma and doctrine, and if it did not then it was altered. This is why the Dead Sea scrolls were kept out of the way for so long. But that is the New Testament and the subsequent writings seen above. What about the Old Testament? The writings of the Jews?

Old Testament original copies exist with columns of numbers on every page. This was instituted so that when copied the figures could be totalled on how many words, verses, expressions and combinations of words were there. This was called Massorah, and it prevented a single word from being missed out or added in. Mistakes were easily picked up and any roll found to be different in any way was discarded. Not one of the ancient or more modern copies of any other texts, such as Plato's Republic, has anything like this kind of security system. Backed up by religious fervour and you have one of the most reliable copying methods in the world.

The discovery of the Dead Sea Scrolls backed up this magnificent almost error free copying methodology with over 500 books having been reconstructed from the fragments. One of these was the book of Isaiah which has now been dated scientifically to 125 BC. This is still the very same text we have in our modern Isaiah. Still, many more Old Testament writings have been found elsewhere even older than that; they too are the same.

We can glimpse upon just how conscientious the Jews were when we look at just a few of the rules that applied to the copyists: -

The scrolls must have been made from animal skins prepared by a Jew in the synagogue and be ceremonially clean.

The amount of columns, lines etc must be the same throughout the entire textual copy.

If even three words were written without an underline the copy was ineffectual.

Nothing could be written from memory, not even a letter.

The copyist should wear complete Jewish dress and should have previously washed his entire body.

Nobody could interrupt him, not even a King.

The names of god should have been written with a newly dipped pen.

One thread between each consonant, 9 consonants between each and every new section, 3 lines between every book.

In this, we can see just how the Jews revered their scriptures and rules.

Now let us look at the secular writings.

Herodotus wrote in 480-425BC. The earliest copy of his writings we have is 1300 years later in 900AD. We only have 8 copies.

Plato wrote in 427-347BC. The earliest copy is 900AD with only 7 copies.

Aristotle wrote in 384-322BC. The earliest copy is 1100AD with only 5 copies.

Caesar wrote 58-50BC. The earliest copy is 850AD with 10 copies.

Now, how does this compare with the New Testament?

Sir Frederick Kenyon - a staunch Christian - said that the New Testament is three times more reliable than any secular text, including Marlowe and Shakespeare. The reason? The New Testament texts were originally written around 50-90AD the earliest complete copies we have are around 330AD. But there is the amazing fact; we have over 5500 copies. Compare that with the examples of secular writings above and we have some pretty good evidence for their reliability. We also have strong evidence that these new Jews were really on a massive marketing push. Fully determined to get their message across on a huge scale. They obviously understood how to get across to their audience.

A.T. Robertson in "An Introduction to Textual Criticism of the New Testament"

"There are some 8000 manuscripts of the Latin Vulgate and at least 1000 for other earlier editions. Add over 4000 Greek manuscripts and we have 13000 manuscripts of portions of the New Testament." So not 5500, but 13000!

J.W. Montgomery in "History and Christianity."

"To be sceptical of the resultant text of the New Testament is to allow all of classical antiquity to slip into obscurity."

The Third edition of the Encyclopaedia Britannica

"...if we deny the authenticity of the New Testament we may with a thousands times greater propriety reject all other writings in the world."

Howard Vos, "Can I Trust the Bible?"

"...the reliability of the New Testament is infinitely stronger than that for any other record of antiquity."

Josh McDowell and Don Stewart in "Answers to Tough Questions."

"Fortunately the problem is not the lack of evidence."

Prof F. F. Bruce in "The New Testament Documents: Are They Reliable?"

"And if the New Testament were a collection of secular writings, their authenticity would generally be regarded as beyond all doubt."

Sir Frederick Kenyon in "The Bible and Archaeology."

"Both the authenticity and the general integrity of the books of the New Testament may be regarded as finally established."

Werner Keller in "The Bible as History."

"The Bible is right after all."

So, can the texts be believed? The answer has to be yes. But, and a very big but, they are to be believed in how they were meant to be. That is, simply, as analogies, fables, myths, human truths, warnings and basic controlling propaganda for the masses. There is just as much evidence, if not more, to prove that the Bible is as reliable as Plato, however we do not take everything Plato says as being 'gospel'. And neither should we the Bible. It was meant for an age, not all ages. We simply have to take out of ourselves any feelings or emotions that we have attached to the Bible, whether good feelings or bad feelings. The reason is simple. If we are to view the Bible as an historical document then we must see it from a purely logical and unbiased point of view. We must not see it as the word of god, forever laid down for our guidance. We must not see it as purely propaganda either. We must view it from a balanced perspective. This is obviously impossible for all of us, and yet we must consciously try to do so. The same applies to all the other religious documents of the world, the Koran included. What the above people quoted have in common is a biased opinion towards Christianity. The point being made is simple. That it does not matter whether you are a Doctor, Professor, Lawyer, Archaeologist or any other kind of expert. If you have an emotional attachment to the subject in a biased way then you cannot see through the evidence clearly. You attach an emotion to all the evidence and seek proof for your emotional attachment. The above so-called experts are right when they say that there is a lot of evidence to support the historicity of the texts, they are wrong to say that the literalisms of the texts are true. If it were true that Jesus walked on water, then it would also be true to say that Atlantis existed as Plato asserted or that the Wizard Merlin really did produce magic. The texts do exist, are historically dateable and do give us an insight into the time and people. But do they tell the truth?

Resurrection

Lord Darling, one time Lord Chief Justice of England wrote, "..there exists such overwhelming evidence, positive and negative, factual and circumstantial, that no intelligent jury in the world can fail to bring in a verdict that the resurrection story is true."

Is it true? Well I do not intend to go over too much old ground, which has already been well trodden. A good read on the subject as stated earlier, is by Frank Morison in "Who moved the stone?". This is however, a Christian book and biased, it should be read in balance and taken with such books as The Shining Ones and Bloodline of the Holy Grail to enable a more balanced perspective.

The one major area which would make Christianity fall, is the resurrection. If, however, the resurrection had never happened at all, because Jesus did not actually die on the cross, then we would be into the arena of altering the history of the western world.

There have been literally hundreds of modern-day magicians or tricksters who have claimed and proven that today they too could pull off the illusion of the resurrection. Without doubt, the efficiency and skill of those people two thousand years ago was tremendous. If we are to believe that they could produce such an awe inspiring set of documents now known as the Bible then we must also believe them capable of such a plot. The intricacies of the Bible and those books still kept out of Holy Scripture are fascinating. I have spoken to endless Christians and Jews alike who feel that the Spirit of god has spoken to them every time they have experienced a new revelation from the Bible.

This was the writers' intention, and it shows an almost unparalleled, unique intelligence. The reason for such immense knowledge is simple. The Shining Ones (a unique and ancient secret brotherhood discovered by myself - see The Shining Ones, www.radikalbooks.com) are behind all religions and have been around for a long time. They organised great centres of learning. They travelled extensively between continents, passed on learning, discussed new movements and discovered new ways all the time. They would have had meetings in which they discussed movements in world opinion, in the various differences between cultures and would have gradually implemented the same controls.

The apostles were not poor people as we have been led to believe. They were quite the opposite. They had no need to work hard for a living, and they had a faith, which moved them forward. They had years of learning under their belt. Jesus was not ready for his ministry until he was thirty, which shows a long-term training implementation in process. We can see from the same periods involved with Buddha and Mahavira that they too probably underwent similar training periods for their role as messiah.

Jesus was perfectly aware of the plot; he shows this in the scriptures when it is said that he knew that the crucifixion was coming. He could rely on his men completely; they were a professional group who had all the plans in place. The stage ready, all which was awaited, was the leading actor. He rode upon a white donkey into Jerusalem with palm branches scattered on the ground as a carpet for the coming Lord. The palm itself is symbolic of several important myths. Firstly, it was the sign of the Flaming Column found on the coinage of Carthage, in the foreground was a great horse. The palm also stood for fire and, even more in keeping with our story here, the Tree of Life. The leaves were never changing and in this they signified the unchangeable lord.

The Phoenicians also held the palm in high esteem, and their coinage displayed the healing serpent coiled around its trunk. The 'Baal Tamar' meant 'Lord of the Palm' and 'Tamar' means 'resplendent Sun Fire'. In Greek, 'palm' is 'phoenix' which has obvious connotations with the resurrected Light or Fire of god. This palm spreading activity may or may not have actually occurred, it may simply have been the disciples playing out their plan and symbolically informing the people of Jerusalem that this was the Christ. After he entered the Temple, Jesus did not find too much of a stir and we find in Mark's Gospel that nothing much occurred. In fact, the disciples were reprimanded for causing a disturbance (Luke). Therefore Jesus went on to Bethany. The prophecies that the messiah would not be recognised came true, and the total rejection of the people for the expected messiah was complete. It was not surprising that he was not recognised. He had spent little time in Jerusalem and was, after all, an Essene, with a group of anti-establishment spies in tow. The people were not expecting symbolism in their messiah, they were expecting force. As history has shown, force, in conjunction with the messiah, has been highly unsuccessful. Any attempt to take power by force, before or after Jesus, proved impossible.

The people did group behind the self-proclaimed messiahs, but never in enough strength to ensure a lasting self-rule. With Jesus, the plan was not a power attempt by force, it was one aimed at the mind and the soul via subtle symbolism.

The next step was for the 'assassin', Judas, to make his move and bring the Priests of the Temple into the knowledge of Jesus' struggle for power. This had the desired effect and the play was truly begun. At this stage, there was no turning back. Next, the Last Supper, the story of so many Gnostic traditions, was planned. In this alone we can see how rich these people were. In one of the most hectic towns of the area, at the busiest time of the year, Jesus and his entourage took their supper in what must have been a huge room. Symbolically, it was an Upper Room, pertaining to the Heavens, and the taking of a meal was reminiscent of the ancient practice of eating on top of mounds.

Here, we have to ask; if Jesus was supposed to move to Bethany after his entrance into Jerusalem, then why is he suddenly back there again? The answer is simple. The Qumran community left Jerusalem and set up in or around Qumran. This new 'Vatican' was called Jerusalem also.

They began the ritual of the Feast of the Messiah or 'Last Supper', which just so happened to be at the same time as the Passover, because the tradition had stayed with the Essene.

Close by there was a place known as 'Mount of Olives', an old monastery. These similarities of names to those of Jerusalem are no surprise. When the English immigrated to the Americas they too started to name the new places with the names of their old land (York/New York etc.). That night, Jesus prayed alone in the place known as Gethsemane and in obvious symbolism showed how he was the messiah. He endured the darkness, where his disciples could not. The act of being alone before a sacrifice is one typical of the Shaman, who would be alone to talk with the spirits before any such practice.

Judas betrayed Jesus as specified in the plan and reveals the Gnostic tradition that it is the self which lets us down, and it is the self which can save us. The trial was short, due to the fact it was a mock trial, under Essene influence and that Pontius Pilate was given power to execute this man. In all the writings regarding Pontius Pilate the stark fact comes across that he had no dislike for Christ and in fact wanted to let him go as he had done nothing wrong. The priests, however, pressed for his execution under the law of the Gentiles. There would be no point in executing him themselves, people would obviously know it to be a fraud and never believe him to be resurrected. The crucifixion had to be public and properly authentic. The sacrifice on the Tree took place.

On the two trees either side (significantly, three in all) were members of the group also placed there as part of the plot. In the books discovered at Nag Hammadi, we find the discourse known as The Second Treatise of the Great Seth. In this we find the words of Jesus, after his crucifixion, 'As for my death - which was real enough to them - it was real to them because of their own...blindness.' We also find a certain Simon of Cyrene who was the one to switch with either Christ himself of one of the others during the walk along the 'way of sorrows' (Via Dolorosa). It may have been Simon the Magi (magician), who was also involved in the deceit, and much has been written regarding this Passover Plot already. We must not forget that it is still an Islamic belief that Jesus did not die on the cross.

It is sufficient for us to say that the following occurred. Either Jesus or Simon the Magi was switched with Simon the Cyrene. A mixture of gall and vinegar was issued to Jesus on the Tree and this had the effect of providing unconsciousness (gall is snake venom and vinegar is poor or soured wine, both symbolically significant items).

Normally, any crucifixion would take at least five days to kill someone. This time Jesus appeared dead within hours and he was taken down and given into the hands of his brother, Joseph of Arimathea.

Joseph was an honourable member of the Sanhedrin and a secret disciple of Christ. He had inherited his father's title of the name 'Joseph' because Gabriel had already issued Jesus his title. Jesus was David, the kingly title, and James his brother was Joseph, the next in line to the title. In this, James was the Crown Prince which translates as 'Rama-Theo' (Divine Highness) he was therefore Joseph of Arimathea (his father's title and crown prince). There is now no confusion as to why Pilate should hand over the body of Jesus to a stranger. Jesus and the other two were taken away to the family tomb which had already been rigged with sufficient escape holes.

Keeping watch over the cave-tomb were angels; the men with official authority. Indeed, those who visited the tomb actually thought that these angels were just ordinary people. If anything, these angels were guarding against spectators and hiding the fact that a conjuring trick was in progress and were most likely to have been Essenes as they were dressed in white and it is known that the Essene were excellent medicine men. In John 19:39, 'He (Joseph) was joined by Nicodemus, who brought with him a mixture of myrrh and aloes, more than half a hundredweight'. Later, Mary of Magdala (the wife of Jesus) said, 'They have taken the Lord out of his tomb.' First Nicodemus brings myrrh and aloes and then, Jesus is 'gone' because 'they' have taken him. Myrrh is a sedative and brings pain relief. The juice taken from aloes is a powerful medicine used to expel unwanted poisons, such as snake venom, from the body's system. Together they were precisely the tools needed by any good 'medicine man' such as Simon or Nicodemus. A great earthquake and an angel appeared. That is, two people appeared, and Simon the young man in a white robe had made their plan come true. The cast of the whole play had brought about one of the world's greatest mysteries, which is still with us today. This was a physical enactment of a spiritual and Gnostic belief. A pagan ideology of the resurrected self, brought to real life in a passion play realism. The deep and long held Gnostic belief becoming reality in a literal way and taken literally, incorrectly, when it was simply meant to be symbolic.

In traditional Shaman style, Jesus then showed he had brought back the power. Flying was a key aspect of this Shamanistic practice as he flew to heaven at the 'Ascension'. Three days after crucifixion his wounds were healed by 'Marham-i-Isa' (Ointment of Jesus), a salve referred to in old medicinal papers and in all likelihood one sold by the Essene to the populace. As we would expect, his return was promised and as we shall see a new leader was chosen by a later Gabriel.

The symbolism of the whole story of Jesus Christ is the richest on the planet and worthy of a much greater study than allowed here. The point is that for two thousand years we have followed this story as literal truth, then we altered slightly and modern rationalism made us see it in the sense of 'good teaching', and now we must see it in the context of not just this good teaching but also a deeper teaching. Within your old Bible, stuffed in the bottom drawer or up in the attic, there are pages of real truth, pages of the real history of mankind. That same history has been hidden from us by the tabloid garbage of the official historians. There is more to history than the kings and queens, the wars and battles, the famines and gold rushes. Behind all power bases there is another story; the story of the ones who do the work in the background and take no credit, the ones who manipulate and cajole those in the public eye.

What we have seen, for the first time in some detail, is the working of the Shining Ones to bring about change. Never before in the history of the Shining Ones had they attempted such a radical departure from the normal low key secretive ways. This operation was huge; the secrets had to be tied up, a specific spy training school had to be employed and for almost the first time these Shining One trainees were to take leading roles. Not only that, decades were wasted trying desperately to establish the correct lineage for the whole thing to come to fruition. Whether the plans went correctly the whole way or not is another matter. The point is that change was brought about. It seems from the historical settings that the Shining Ones, Moses, Abraham, Buddha, Mahavira, and as we have seen a much larger list, had learnt much from their ancient dealings. The skill, knowledge, sheer determination and bravery of such a plot must have seemed daunting at times. But with the military chiefs, intelligence officers, assassins, teachers, ministers, princes, Baptists, Gentiles and magicians, there were sufficient numbers of highly skilled operatives in and off the field to enable a complicated plot like this to be worked out. If ever there was a 'mission impossible' then this was it.

However, one peculiar aspect of the resurrection myth is the number of highly intelligent men and women who have tackled it. This is due to the sheer weight of evidence on both sides. Lord Lyndhurst said, "Such evidence has never broken down." and Professor Sir Norman Anderson said that the empty tomb itself stood as a veritable rock of evidence.

Christians and non-Christians alike agree that the resurrection of Christ is one of the most attested to facts in the ancient world. It is the very matter, which would simply make Christianity fall. And yet there are now hundreds of books out there with all manners of alternative views and evidence opposing the factual idea of the resurrection, and yet Christianity still survives. We still fail to understand the power of faith.

St Paul tells us in 1 Corinthians 15:6 that over 500 people witnessed the resurrected Christ. Many of these people were still alive when Paul wrote his account and could have easily testified to any lie that was told; yet they did not. Of course people saw Christ, resurrected, walking abroad, this they would have seen whether he had died, or not. In the secular writings of Josephus we hear that "They reported that he had appeared to them three days after his crucifixion and that he was alive; accordingly he was perhaps the Messiah concerning whom the prophets have recounted wonders." These writings of Josephus are however under much doubt. It is highly likely that they were altered to suite the growing Christian beliefs.

So what is the Christian view of exactly what happened to Christ? What evidence do they put forward to oppose the growing historian's view of the 'plot'?

After Christ had been crucified, he was placed in a tomb and a guard set of either Jews or Romans. The first people to find the tomb empty however were the women who had actually watched his burial. Next came Peter and John who ran to the tomb. The guards then reported it to the Jewish authorities and even the Sanhedrin admitted to the fact.

We also find that history tells us nothing of the veneration of the burial place of Christ. This is unusual unless we admit the fact that he was somehow moved from that place. There was indeed, no body to venerate. He had either been resurrected or the whole thing had been a simple magic trick.

So the tomb was empty. Now it is a question as to what happened to the body, or person.

Could the disciples have stolen the body? Firstly they would have committed a serious offence legally and would have been hunted down. This is of course if the body had been buried anywhere near Jerusalem. There is now strong evidence to suggest that the whole plot happened near Qumran, and therefore the whole section of evidence surrounding the Jerusalem story will fall.

There is, however, no evidence to suggest that the disciples were arrested or victimised for stealing the body.

Christians also point out that the disciples left behind the burial clothes, pointing out that Jesus no longer needed these earthly clothes. There is evidence, released by myself that discredits this idea however. There is a huge amount of evidence to show that Jesus was perceived as a serpent god. Snakes regularly moult their skin and the ancient saw this as a symbol of rejuvenation. Many of the Essene were members of a Theban cult called the Ophites. These were medicine men, skilled in extending life and treating the ill. Ophite comes from the Greek word for snake, Ophis. This was an Egyptian cult and the Qumran Essene was closely linked with their brethren in the Egyptian Essene order. The sloughing of the skin and the leaving behind of the pre-resurrected clothes are therefore symbolic of this rejuvenation.

Christians also ask what the motive could possibly have been to have faked the resurrection. They claim that the disciples would have been seen as frauds, which is highly likely had the people known that the whole thing had been a fraud. Everything the disciples preached rested around the resurrection. It was all too important for them to be seen as frauds. Most of the disciples, it is claimed, died for their beliefs. Many modern day members of the Masons and other similar secret societies have little knowledge of the true ancient and historical intentions of their cults, only a chosen few are aware. The same must simply have been true of the disciples. Not all of them would have known of the plot, even if just purely for the sake of secrecy.

Maybe Christ was still alive when he was placed in the tomb? Again the Christians have an answer. The Romans, they say, knew how to kill and did a very good job of it. They were trained in murder and crucifixion was second nature to many. In the severe beating that Jesus supposedly received prior to being hung on the cross, he went through something that many died in receiving. If then, the asphyxiation death of crucifixion were not the final blow to Jesus then the lance that pierced his side would have been. This released a flow of blood and water; supposedly typical of the effects produced from a dead man when pierced. Professor of Surgery at Bristol

University, Rendle Short tells us "..a condition of acute dilation of the stomach may have developed, and the spear wound drew watery fluid from the stomach and blood from the heart and great vessels of the Thorax... Needless to say, such a wound would be instantly fatal if the victim was not already dead..."

Firstly, if the plot had actually taken place in Qumran, then it was simply under symbolised Roman edict that Jesus had been sentenced. The actual plot was carried out by the Essene. Secondly, the lance in the side was also symbolic of serpent worship. According the Greek myth the left-hand side of the serpent when pierced issues forth poison, the right hand side the elixir of life. Christ could have been symbolically issuing forth the elixir of life - for further information see my new book.

Resurrection Notes: - Rebirth - Bhagavad Gita, 'I have been born many times', Bible 'You must be born again', Egyptian Book of the Dead, 'I have the power to be born a second time'. Christian belief in reincarnation before 500AD. Egyptian rebirth rituals abound. Magi believed in reincarnation. Zoroaster, Osiris, Horus, Adonis, Dionysus, Hercules, Hermes, Baldur and Quertzalcoatl all descended into hell and were risen again on the third day. Vishnu said 'Every time that religion is in danger and that iniquity triumphs I issue forth for the defence of the good and the suppression of the wicked; for the establishment of justice I manifest myself from age to age.' Resurrection is all part of Mithraism, the Orphic mysteries and Isis worship (and not surprisingly these were the very religions, Christianity had to compete with and were inspired by).

Conclusion

Basically then, in conclusion we can only prove a couple of things.

That the actual literary texts of the Bible are true in as much as they are one of the most historically backed texts we have from antiquity. However, we do not believe that Horus had the head of a falcon and was a sun god just because hieroglyphs show him that way. In the same way we cannot in first light believe that Jesus cast out demons into swine or was resurrected from the dead.

We have shown that there is much of historical interest within the Bible and that we should not always throw away everything before examining the data thoroughly. There is, however, no evidence for the existence of god. There are many ways to take the more mythological texts than on purely face value.

Flood or Fantasy?

What do the following civilisations have in common?

Babylonia, Israel, Persia, Egypt, Greece, India, Teuton's, Ahts Indians, Brazil, Polynesia, Tibet, Kashmir, Lithuania, Carib, Mexico, Bogota, Peru, Sumeria, Mesopotamia, Australia and Britain?

The answer, they all have in their folklore the peculiar myth of a universal flood. In reality nearly every culture on the Earth has some element of a flood deep within their misty pasts. This may be some kind of Jungian archetype or as Dr Aaron Smith pointed out may be actual historical accuracy. He found 80000 works in 72 languages that had some component of a flood. Of these 80000 works there were 70000 that mentioned the remains of the Ark.

Can this be some strange quirk of chance? Or was there a flood that so impressed itself upon the world, that we remember it in the subconscious of our national inheritance? What does this evidence offer us in the way of proof for god? Does it prove that the word of god is correct? Can we suddenly trust his word? Or do we take the whole thing as if it were some fairy tale child's fantasy? We shall examine the testimony of witnesses in the following pages.

Do all the myths around the globe say the same thing?

Quite simply, they are remarkably similar. Take for example the Babylonian Epic of Gilgamesh. In it we find a man called Utnapishtim who was called upon by the god Ea to "..build a ship; abandon wealth, seek after life; scorn possessions, save thy life. Bring up the seed of all kinds of living things into the ship: the ship, which thou shalt build. Let its dimensions be well measured." This was done, and Utnapishtim left his tale for us to read, whether we take it literally or as fable.

As if by pure coincidence this story of the Babylonian Noah fits with the Genesis account and many believe that the Jews took the Gilgamesh Epic as their starting point for the Biblical account. The Gilgamesh narrative says, "I brought into the ship my whole family and kinsfolk." Genesis 7:1 says "Go into the ark, you and your

whole family." In fact, many of the things mentioned by Utnapishtim fit entirely with the scientific records as well.

We have described for us great cyclones of tropical areas and massive tidal waves. This leaves everything covered in a layer of mud and completely flat. Meteorologist's now believe that this epic is based on an eyewitness account of a great flood. They say that it was, however, localised, and when the word universal is used, they believe this means the universe as far as the Babylonians were concerned.

When we look deeper into the world's myths we find that the same thing applies to the Hopi Indians and Inca's of South America. In fact we find that this similarity is also found in Greece, Assyria, Palestine, Mexico and many more. Could the story of this localised universal flood have been handed around? Could the world have remembered a flood, which seemed universal? Could all of the world's flood myths have come from one original source? That of the original Noah?

What scientific evidence is there for a flood?

There is a relatively new science called Polaromagnetism. This reveals proof within the magnetism of rocks that the axis of which the world turns has altered. This is why we now have 365 days to our annual cycle and not 360 as there were originally. Confirmation that there was a 360-day calendar is found in such ancient civilisations as Hindu, Greek, Babylonian, Peruvian, Mayan and Egyptian cultures.

The theory states that there was a re-alignment of the inner magnetic core of the Earth and the poles, which caused a sudden, swell of seawater, plentiful enough to swamp the Earth. It emerges that the water from the poles would have sped around the globe and have reached in excess of 300 mile per hour. Oceans would have altered direction and would have raised up from the deep, just as the Biblical record states. This in turn would have caused great periods of rainfall with unparalleled proportions, maybe even 40 days and 40 nights!

This evidence is found in fossil records deposited on beeches and especially in the Andes, where there has been found 12000 feet high, just such fossil records. Corel beds are said to be at peculiar angles and those ancient civilisations saw a different pole star. When this scientific information is placed alongside the historical findings it cannot be denied as being evidence for a massive flood. The question is what caused it? Was it god? Condemning us for our sins? Or was it a possibly a comet or asteroid hitting the Earth with such force as to cause it to come into such calamity? If it were a comet, did god send it?

What is the historical evidence?

It has been much disputed whether fossil fuels were formed by gradual or catastrophic means. The existence of such fuels could be good proof for a universal flood, as there are massive deposits around the globe and some say seem to have been from the same periods. We all know that when a fish dies it floats to the surface and lies on its side. It then proceeds to decompose slowly and separate. The various parts falling to the sea bed. Yet if these fish were to be fossilised in a perfect state then they would have to die instantaneously, such as in a violent tidal wave or deluge of mud. We find around the planet, millions upon millions of just such fossilised fish, packed tightly into the various strata. These fish died in huge shoals as if crushed by the sheer weight of some terrible flood.

Similar claims can be made for most animals we find fossilised, and this is claimed by Christians, Jews and Muslims around the globe to be the case. One case they point out as perfect evidence of this is Carnegie Hill in Nebraska.

At this one location there was in excess of 9000 animals, all of which are not now native to America. The evolutionist theory states that these animals had all been feeding around the lake when they all suddenly fell in, either one by one or en masse. Yet, in the surrounding hilly area, geologists have dug down the same distance and found the same evidence. This means that the animals feeding at the edge must have jumped hundreds of miles to have piled themselves up in the centre of the lake. Not likely. Is this evidence therefore, for a worldwide disaster? Could very well be.

However, there is much contention about the fossil evidence providing proof for the flood. All that can be said for sure is that both explanations for the fossil evidence could be true. It does not have to be only one explanation. Both gradual accumulation and natural catastrophe are true. Over the millions of years that the Earth has existed, all number of catastrophes could have struck. From comet hits to the very crusts of our planet deciding to alter course, all things are possible. The fact remains a universal or large localised flood is highly likely, and within the period of man's early period. There is new evidence coming to light as I write this book, that man may have existed alongside the late dinosaurs.

Biblically god could have just flooded the known world or the inhabited world at the time. After all, what need is there to flood parts of the globe that have no human sin? We should remember the motive for flooding the Earth. To stop mankind's sinful ways, so that we could start afresh. Pointless therefore, to flood some far off land that was not inhabited by humans.

So, there is sufficient evidence to prove a flood of some magnitude. What evidence do the religious among use for their purposes?

When examining sediment in the Gulf of Mexico, a dramatic change in the salinity at a distant point in the past was found. It turned out to be a symptom of the melting North American ice cap. This melting in turn produced a great tidal flow around the globe. However, the Gulf of Mexico is not on it's own. It is joined with many other areas such as the Euphrates River, which has in the surrounding area ten feet thick flood clay.

Dr C. L. Wooley, who discovered the Egyptian flood clay wrote, "..is the flood of the book of Genesis! ...in no other way can I interpret the facts... We were loath to believe that we had obtained confirmation of the deluge of Genesis, but there is no doubt about it now."

Other flood evidence much like the above has also been discovered in England, Wales, Scotland, African continent, China, France, America and Java. Obviously not all such evidence is from the universal flood, but it highlights the existence of a lot of evidence supporting the Biblical account.

An ancient cuneiform which resides in the Ashmolean Museum in Oxford states on line 39, "The Deluge came up!", this correlates to the Biblical account "springs of the great deep burst forth". All the other lines on this ancient cuneiform have been found to be factual, chronological orders of kings and royal lineages. It follows that the two lines regarding the flood should also be true.

Fossils of sea creatures have been found on mountaintops all over the world. Animals that do not spend their time on mountain tops. Fragments of man and animal bone mixed together. Mammoths, lions, camels and horses, all together, as if caught in some great catastrophe. In Siberia scientists have found many frozen Mammoths, caught as if the world suddenly changed. These are so prolific that scientists are now famous for holding Mammoth burger events, as the meat is still fresh.

Zoologists claim that the distribution of plant life is evidence for a worldwide flood sometime in the Earth's history.

There are many more historical evidences, which would require a whole book, and there are many books. However I will end by briefly mentioning evidence from the frequency in the genes of specific blood groups. This evidence alongside migration evidence gives a unique insight into the common ancestry of man, post flood, and how his racial family tree can supposedly be traced back to one single origin and location, just where the Ark is said to have come to rest. A strange coincidence, or proof for the Ark?

So what about the Ark?

The Bible gives us surprisingly the exact measurements for the Ark. It was 437.5 feet long, 72.92 feet in width and 43.7 feet high. There was a total deck area of 95700 square feet. The volume capacity was 1396000 cubic feet with a gross tonnage of 13960 ton's. It would have been able to carry 4522 modern rail road boxcars, each of which would carry 125000 sheep. Therefore all the creatures known today would fit into 150 cars.

There was no shortage of space. Not only that, but we must remember with animal husbandry today we have developed many more kinds of animals within their species. Frank Lewis Marsh illustrated how over 500 varieties of peas had been developed from just one since 1700ad. So there we have evidence that whoever wrote down the specification for the ship had been very thorough and had an understanding of the worlds resources which would have needed saving. Although not as large as this, there were ships similar in design well within the timescale of Noah. In fact remains of such ships have been discovered.

The Ark is said to have come aground on the mountain ranges of Ararat in Turkey. At the foot of the actual mount Ararat lies a small village called Bayzit. The villagers here have for centuries held the belief that there are the remains of a huge ship up in the mountains. Of course this belief could easily have stemmed from Christian belief over the centuries permeating into the mindset of the locals. From monks, travellers and crusades, such myths are created. It has been seen by the Archdeacon of Jerusalem, a first world war Russian pilot, a search party of Tsar Nicholas and several photographs have been taken by Russian and American pilots. These photographs led to the latest expedition and interesting discoveries, which did indeed lead to an excavation of a huge ship like shape, which lies on the very mountain ranges in question.

The ship is, surprisingly, just about the right size. Both American archaeologists and the Turkish authorities are undergoing strenuous attempts to research the area under what are obviously difficult conditions.

Conclusion

So from the above study what can we draw out and claim as our elusive proof?

Well, we must turn towards the Christian again and ask him what he claims to be his truth.

Firstly, he says that we do have evidence for a flood at least. This we agree. Secondly, that a large amounts of animal, human and plants life was wiped out and we had to start again. We do not necessarily agree, although it could be true, we are still awaiting the scientist's viewpoint on this.

Thirdly, they state that the Ark is a reality and not a child's fairy tale. We could concede and say that this is a distinct possibility. However, does it prove the existence of god? I don't think so.

Christians say that if this part of the Bible is true, then why is it that the rest is not? All the facts fit the tale. Maybe we should look at the other books in detail, from a scientific and historical point of view to see if they too hold remarkable truths. Lack of faith, we are told, can come from lack of knowledge. Lack of knowledge can also result in faith.

OK, so we are forced to re-think that old school room story of Noah in the light of this evidence. But, I ask, why should evidence for an ancient flood and boat, be evidence for the existence of god? Just because it talks about Noah, the flood and the Ark in the Bible does not make the rest of the Bible truth. If it did, then the rest of the Epic of Gilgamesh would also be true, and there are some pretty fanciful things in there that would need serious explanation.

The Biblical flood is, at the end of the day, just simply a universal archetype, a memory of some past disaster, which affected the known world. It is not evidence that god decided to punish us and wipe us all out. It is, however, socially and historically interesting, but that is where it stays.

Science or Sci-Fi?

Science is probably one of the biggest and most controversial issues to write about in a book about god. It is a more philosophical subject than people like to believe. Indeed, beliefs about science are stronger or as strong as religion. Just like religion or politics, everybody has an opinion on it. From the devout who just take the scientist on their word to the doubting Thomas whom constantly needs proof of what the scientist claims.

Of course to answer every religious-science question would take a book bigger than mine, however I do believe it is time to take a balanced look at the whole thing. My reason is simple, there are many Christian and religious books out there all claiming science as their friend, all the time only giving one side of the story. It is time to check the science specific evidence that Christians claim for their beliefs.

Firstly, they claim that the argument between science and religion is a fallacy.

The word, science, means branch of knowledge, requiring systematic study and method, dealing with substances, life and natural law. In short, it is the mechanics of life. The how we live, not why. We have two very basic choices for the 'why'. Philosophy or religion.

The word, religion, means to believe in the existence of a controlling power and the worship thereof. The why we live, not how.

We can see from their definitions that they are not even comparable, yet we appear to make them battle out issues which we say cross over into each other's arenas. We do not seem to do this with philosophy, as this does not become an area of highly charged emotions and has few doubters. Basically, philosophy does try to explain why we live; it is open for discussion and not closed off to outside influence. Religion alternatively is closed and needs defending against an ever-changing world of science and facts.

Both fields of religion and science are almost esoteric in essence. Each one is intended for a person with special knowledge or insight. These insights may sometimes have regard for the same issue, however, each one views that issue from a unique angle.

The books of the world faiths were not meant to be scientific. Indeed had they started out telling mankind about photons, protons and quarks, then the ancients would not have understood. Instead many of the mysteries were explained in language that they could understand. Instead, if god does exist, then it may be that he covered all 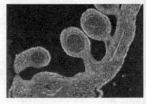 the angles pretty well. It seems that he simplified the structure and chronological order of scientific creation events. It could be that if we read the Biblical creation events in chronological order alongside the scientific viewpoint, that the language differs, but the events are the same.

The book of books, as the Christians call it, was never meant to tell us exactly how things happened, but why. It is our ancient ancestor's method of understanding the world around him and in this context it is believable. Science is our modern interpretation of our beliefs. It is highly likely that our descendants will look back on our belief and mock. Scientists give us their hard worked out theories and ask us to believe them. Is essence, to have faith in their stated theory. The theories are based upon the facts as we see them now, just as the ancients had beliefs built around the world as they saw it.

Science is almost as much a religion as Christianity. Almost. We must take into account progress, evolution of the human mind. We are not the same as the ancients because we have developed, learnt and discovered more. Simple beliefs are no longer suitable for our complex minds. However, as we look into the realms of this modern day religion called science we still find that it takes immense amounts of faith and gut feeling. Scientific theories are still changing daily, if religionists changed their scriptures as much as scientists do then religion may have been out of business a long time ago. Faith is built and works on solid structures. An unchanging, unwavering religious structure breeds belief. Long standing implies solidity. Constant change upsets the human mind and brings in doubt.

For instance, Charles Darwin wrote The Origin of Species, his evolutionary theory of selective process. Thousands were converted overnight to this new theory. Of course, science has moved on and changed even this groundbreaking idea, so much so that Darwin may not even recognise evolution, as he understood it. Darwin, however, was even casting huge doubts over his own theory towards the end of his life. His theories, in the blink of an eye, soon became old hat as a new concept entered the market place. No solidity, no unwavering and people began to turn back to the church for their hope. The way of the evolutionist it seemed was

risky, wavering, changing and confused. Although Neo-Darwinism is now the concept popularly accepted as true by many.

So how do we look into the two areas of science and religion without getting bogged down in all the changeable arguments?

Science however flawed by changing ways and commercial funding is still the search for truth, like any religion. The difference is that science at least can be tested in the laboratory. Faith cannot. Where it can fall down though is in theoretical study. This can many times be so profoundly unexplainable that people simply turn off to it as being unbelievable. It needs to be easily understood to be believed. Strangely, this even applies to scientists themselves whom are constantly arguing amongst themselves about their theories, bringing to mind the hundreds of years of arguments between the clergy about their theologies.

Christians, however, say that we can often take the natural world for granted, but we must realise that we are seeing another aspect of god. That this too is his book, to be read and enjoyed. Most of all, to be cared for, just as they protect his word in the Bible. Simple as that. All the problems with the Biblical theology are ignored and a simple smile of faith recovers where doubt creeps in. When we read both of god's books, they say, we can come to a better understanding of what god is. As Einstein once said, "Science without religion is lame, religion without science is blind."

Science is something we have created to explain how things happen through experimentation and observation. The Bible and other religious documents are there to help us understand why. The two 'can' be equal and important.

One of the first problems with science (and religion) is that it is humans who carry out the experiments and write the resultant texts. They still come armed to the teeth with preconceptions and prejudices about what the outcome should be. These are called theories. Most of the time, it must be said, these theories are right. However, poor old nature is often bent this way or that to fit with current beliefs. Nature must fit our idea, our scientific perception. Otherwise we have no answer; we must selectively perceive what we want to perceive. Any theorist who pushes back the boundary of our understanding, for instance on quantum theory, risks sounding even more far fetched than the religionist. This is true of both science and religion.

Let's take a simple analogy. I know (or have a theory) in my own mind that when I turn the kettle on the water will boil. However when the water does not boil I immediately check to make sure that the plug is in, the power is turned on that that there are not other electrical problems. It may have been, however, that water simply does not boil nor needs greater heat than the kettle can provide. It was my prejudice (assuming I had no previous knowledge that water will boil in a kettle from previous experimental results) and theory that water would boil. I did not doubt that the water would boil, instead I searched for other reasons. I know this is a very simple argument, but it serves to show how we can assume our theories, however simple, are correct prior to experimental results.

In an article in the New Scientist (1995) there was research carried out by Stanley Miller of the University of California at San Diego which went a long way to proving that life could not have started in the heat of the oceans. It was previously believed and theorised that life started in the near to boiling point temperatures of the deep oceanic volcanic vents. This theory and belief came about because scientists thought the early, first organisms to be similar to modern day bacteria which thrive in high temperatures.

Many people believe that the four building blocks of RNA (Ribonucleic Acid - primary agent for transferring information from the genome to the protein synthetic machinery of the cell) could have formed spontaneously on the Earth without outside intervention. Some believe space debris caused the rice cocktail of life.

However, Miller has reported that RNA bases actually break down, not build up, in hot water. Miller stored sterilised solutions of the bases at zero degrees centigrade and at boiling point for several months. At boiling point, the four bases showed such degeneration that they would have been lost in a matter of decades - not long enough for life to evolve.

The solution stored at freezing point, on the other hand, would have had half-lives of thousands and even millions of years.

This new research provides a remarkable proof for the theory that we still know relatively little about our origins. And yet, we are told to believe every natural history programme, which tells us categorically where we came from. A scientist can never by experiment tell me why I live, why the big bang and evolution are our origins, or explain why we feel love, hate and fear. We can suggest why we feel love, hate and fear, based upon theories of evolution. We can attribute mechanical ideas around love, but why was love chosen and by whom?

Gerald Joyce of the Scripps Research Institute in La Jolla, California says that it is more likely that first forms of life did not need RNA. Who is correct? Both sets of scientists are highly esteemed, well funded and neither knows the truth in certainty. Maybe god started life? It could be just as feasible. It has more 'human' reason to it. God would, after all, explain the why part of our conundrum. But then, it is also just as feasible that life erupted from nothing or even that life has always been - it just needs the bending of perception.

Sometimes scientists can make the facts fit their theories and anything that crops up as a misdemeanour within the experiment is classed as being out of line and is discarded as worthless, when it may have been, laterally speaking, just what they were looking for.

An example of this is the famous experimental scientist Hertz. When conducting experiments on the speed of radio waves he presumed that the size and shape of a given room did not matter and that objects placed within it would have no effect on the experiment. It was only later, after his death, that it was discovered that the size, shape and objects in a room did indeed matter to the experiment, thus drastically altering the results through rebounding interference. This may now seem a simple problem, but to Hertz it was ground breaking. There are, today, experiments which modern day scientists are conducting that are also ground breaking and which are being approached via prejudices in just the same way.

Maybe we should remember that the Bible itself has never actually attacked science. Indeed, science has never likewise, attacked the Bible. It is the humans who come between them and put them at odds due to their own prejudices. According to many scientific Christians the two can work together. They say that we must move away from the theory that I am right, therefore, you must be wrong, attitude. It has caused wars and battles over centuries. Maybe if we saw them together somehow, we could experiment with at least two prejudices and not just one. Expanding our horizon just a little. Maybe, at least, the human mind would be self satisfied with the created spiritual nature, whilst at least moving the evolution of mankind forward via scientific experimentation.

Christians often point to the theory of Quantum Physics as an answer to this riddle of science and religion working together, even if in theory. It has been suggested that Quantum Physics could prove the existence of a fourth dimension. A dimension outside of time and space. It is a theoretical device which scientists use whenever something does not fit their findings. For illustration, they state that the universe did not start in Real Time, thus solving the problem of uniformity by having a universe that smoothly came into time when it wanted to. They also believe it takes away the need for a god to press the button. Why do these specific scientists take such great pleasure in disproving god? Surely, Christians say, the existence of a fourth dimension would be a suitable location for god? May that's where heaven is?

They say that, just because science can find out about how something happened, it does not mean that god did not make it happen. Just because there was a big bang, does not mean that god did not plant the dynamite. Indeed, no matter what scientists prove about creation, evolution or the end of time, they cannot disprove god. In the same respect, they cannot prove his existence either.

Dr Wilkinson, a PhD in theoretical astrophysics said when speaking about Stephen Hawkins theory on everything, "To claim that such a theory gives full explanation of the universe is incorrect and it in no way disproves the existence of god."

Instead of disproving god, it appears that many scientists are actually converting to god. American Physicist, Freeman Doyle, once said, "The more I examine the universe and study the details of it's architecture, the more evidence I find that the universe in some sense must have known that we were coming."

Professor Stephen Hawkins himself said, "It would be perfectly consistent with all we know to say that there was a being responsible for the laws of physics."

No matter how they word it, they cannot get away from god. It seems that many of the scientific and theoretical discoveries are becoming so profound that the human mind, yet again, has to explain it away as god. One scientist in particular was so convinced by the supposed weight of mathematical evidence for a universal creator that he is now an ordained minister and was prior to that Professor of Mathematical Physics at Cambridge.

There are now so many scientists turning to god because of their discoveries that they have to set up special societies to protect themselves. Indeed, the Scientific Creationists in America recently had evolution theory banned from school classes. This kind of madness is obviously dangerous and holds only the human race back.

It emerges then, that man can reason the workings of a mechanically structured existence and arrive at explanations on how we exist. But when somebody raises the question, why, they are at a loss. Some look at the Bible and claim to have found the answer, others look towards philosophy, and others say they no longer have the need to know why - the question simply has no answer.

However, scientists do not easily believe things, which all along they held to be within the realms of the mystics. They have to collate the evidence and judge, via experiment, what their stated beliefs should be. We will now try to look at the individual questions raised and utilised by Christian Scientists in their defence of their beliefs.

In the Beginning.

The Big Bang Theory

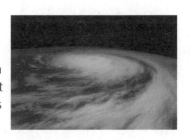

According to science, in simple terms, 10 to 20 billion years ago all matter and energy was concentrated at an immensely hot point which exploded. Since this time the universe has been expanding and cooling.

So what evidence is there for this theory? Light travels at a finite speed. For instance the television pictures transmitted from Apollo 11 took a fraction over 1 second to reach the Earth from the Moon. Now, if we go and look at the distant galaxies with this same information we find that we are looking at images that have taken 10 billion years to get here. From looking at the state of these galaxies and the speed that they are moving, scientists claim to be able to see proof for the big bangs existence.

Now, Einstein stepped onto the scene with his theory of general relativity (although there is much contention as to whether it was actually his idea or not) which takes away absolute time and replaces it with a time that is dependant upon motion. When we put the movement of planetary bodies and general relativity together we get space-time. Time now apparently depended on the shape, size and gravitational position of planetary objects; all these things controlled the rate of flow of time.

When two scientists used Einstein's theory to prove that the universe was expanding by a series of complicated mathematics, the man himself replied, "This circumstance irritates me." He was even prepared to alter his theory, to defend creationism.

Another part of the proof for the big bang theory is redshift. Arno Penzia and Robert Wilson discovered this in 1969 and it is to do with the light waves being emitted from stars and galaxies. When we observe objects that have this redshift coming from them we can say that they are moving away from us at x speed. It is the universal equivalent of a plane passing overhead. On the planes approach it has a higher pitched noise than when it has passed by. This going away noise of planets is entitled redshift. When we have discovered the speed of this redshift we can work backward to the point when all the planets were together and that basically pinpoints the moment of the big bang.

So is the big bang the only theory? No. In 1948 Thomas Gold, Herman Bondi and Fred Hoyle gave the world the steady state theory. This theory proposed a universe, which is still being created in little 'pops' rather than one big bang. As the universe gets bigger the gaps are filled in with new galaxies. A number of scientists were won over and are still split. One physicist stated, "The steady state theory is philosophically the most attractive theory because it least resembles the account given in Genesis."

Ever since the discovery by Arno Penzia and Robert Wilson, most scientists have put their faith, for the time being, in the big bang.

At the time of the introduction of the big bang theory a few scientists opposed it because they disliked the idea of a creating being, and they saw the big bang as proving his existence. They saw that the Genesis account in the Bible matched remarkably with the scientific view.

Science	Genesis
The universe begins as an explosion and is without form.	In the beginning god created the heavens and the earth.
Great flashes of light are abound as protons collide.	And god said Let there be light, and there was light.
Pre-Cambrian era of thick dark soup like steam.	First day began in darkness
Steam condenses into seas	Expanse between waters as they are separated.
Chloroplasts oxidise the rocks and green algae arrives	Dry land appears (rocks) and vegetation sprout to life
The thick effluvium clears to uncover the sun and other lights	Let there be lights in the expanse of sky to separate the day form night.
Post-Cambrian marine life	Let the water teem with living creatures.
Insects take to flight	Winged creatures
Great amphibians and reptilian sea life	Creatures of the sea
Age of mammals and land animals	Let the land produce living animals
Man appeared	Let us make man.

As you can see, without any changes to either science or Genesis the two can run together in the same order. Now, however, we run across the problem of time. How long did it really take the Christian, Judaic or god of Islam to create everything?

The question is do we take the six creation days to mean solar days or creation periods? There are many theories upon this subject and it can get clouded in so much confusion that it takes away from the startling fact of science correlating with Genesis. This one stumps even devout atheists. It brings about the question of whether early man had some scientific understanding of how the order must have been, or he had a direct knowledge of how it all came about from god.

Some Christians have said that the creation days were age-days, and that they could have been many millions of years long. One evidence for this is the suggestion that the sun was not created until the fourth day, in which case the solar days could not have existed for the first three. Also, according to this theory god is still resting from the creation on his seventh day! Which answers a lot of atheistic questions about why god does not do anything about the suffering we all go through.

The Hebrew word used for the day is Yom, as used in Psalm 90:4, "For a thousand years in your sight are like a day that has just gone by..." And again in 2 Peter 3:8, "But do not forget this one thing, dear friends: With the Lord a day is like a thousand years, and a thousands years are like a day." This is repeated again and again throughout the Bible.

Others oppose this however, saying that Genesis does not need to harmonise with science and that the universe just looks more mature. We know from scripture that god supposedly fermented the wine for Jesus in the blink of an eye and that god could just as easily have fermented the universe. However, with such scripture on the thousand year days there seems little need to take this stance. Either way, both theories, age-day and solar day (with seeming age) are in line with the big bang theory and are plausible, as long as you have faith. There are other theories of course, Galaxy days for instance which states that each day is the same as the rotation of a galaxy, that is 360 million years. Could the ancients have worked this one out? They do show a remarkable understanding of the universe with the positioning and mechanics behind stone circles and other great monuments. They have been shown to have taken into account the Earth's shifting polarity and procession. Maybe they worked it out?

A book on the subject, which puts across some Christian biased opinions, is Creation and Evolution by Alan Hayward. The author states categorically, "Of course evolution happened, but it happened with a purpose."

Of course there is also the possibility that scientists have totally the wrong idea. Even as yet they have no explanation for their problem of galaxy formation or how exactly they come together. They have a theory, but as yet, no evidence.

Another suggestion by one eminent scientist was that Genesis could have been

written as a purely topographical and poetic piece of literature with a certain amount of revelation within. This too is possible; it gives Genesis a logical order, with no set timings.

It is easy to see that Genesis could stand the test of science even though it was never meant to be a science book in itself. The big bang now begs the question of causal effect - the who started it all question. This question is not new and a big exponent was Thomas Aquinas in the 13th century.

Some, of course, ask who created god? A reasonable question, but if we use the scientists fourth dimensional theory, we, like them, can fill in this peculiar gap in theology. It is a little like asking where the corners are in the circle. There is no logical answer. In Genesis it states simply, "In the beginning, god...." We are finite beings, as is the universe. All things degrade; we can thank thermodynamics for the answer to this. Some say that god was not the creator until he created. He therefore altered his own existence, his own position in matter. There was no beginning until he began it. Surely, Christians say, if we could answer all the conundrums then we would be gods.

One peculiar idea which comes from the investigation into the big bang beginnings and related happenings is the evidence of balance, commonly known as the Anthropic principle. In fact this idea was so startling to Professor Fred Hoyle of the steady state theory fame, that he said, "Nothing has shaken my atheism as much as this discovery."

Firstly, we have background microwave radiation varying across the whole of our sky by less than 1/30000 parts. This shows us a smooth, uniform and organised universe. Exactly as it ought to be in a created universe. Or indeed, a universe that was now a lot calmer at the start than presently believed.

Secondly, if we take a look at the balance between expansion of the universe and gravitational force we find a perfect and astonishing structure. It is much like blowing up a balloon to the very limit. What this means is, as the universe expands, so the gravitational forces must keep a tight hold on everything. If this were not in such flawless symmetry then all things would be blown apart or crushed in an instant. To be a little more precise the exact balance required is 10 followed by 60 zero's. The chance of getting this balance by luck is remote, but not impossible. The quantum theory of the scientists allows for anything to be possible.

Strangely these peculiar balances carry on right down to the smallest known thing. From the correct mixture of carbon and oxygen for breathing to the mixture of hydrogen and oxygen to produce water. From the distance between the sun and earth to the very natural balance of hunter and hunted on this unusual planet of ours. Our ancient, mystical friends used the hermetic term, as above, so below, microcosm and macrocosm and the golden mean to give language to these remarkable phenomena.

In mathematics we have some extraordinary stability. For instance there are 36 quarks in the universal soup, 360 degrees in a circle, originally 360 days in a year, 360 million-year galaxy cycle and 3600 seconds per hour. Order, however, coming from chaos, does cause mathematical phenomena, and this is just another one of them. Mathematics is behind everything and order, shown by ordered mathematics, is systematic of a thermodynamic balancing from chaos. In other words, it can be explained via scientific theory.

Christians, however, say this whole equilibrium could only have come about through some causal effect. Indeed, thousands of scientists across the planet also say that the universe must have been created. The possibilities, they say, of a universe arriving by accident, out of nothing, with gravitational miracles and balance, and then stumbling upon intelligent life, is so remote that it is farcical. There are however, even more scientists who say that mathematical probabilities now need re-writing, because not only is it possible for life to evolve from nothing, it quite simply has and it is our understanding which is incorrect.

Related Evidence - or just good friends?

Here are a few other pieces of evidence wheeled out by Christians.

1   Job 26:7 states, "He suspends the Earth over nothing."

Many centuries after this statement people around the world still believed all manners of curious things. Elephants, Hercules, Turtles and great pillars held up the mantle of the Earth. Who can blame them? The very thought of the Earth being held aloft by nothing could easily have been seen as equally stupid. It is only now, ever since scientific advancement, that we have been able to see the planet from a different angle, other than from on it. But how did Job know? Was it because he was a man of god? Or was he a great astronomer?

Sounds like a reasonable argument. However, we now know from many ancient stone monuments, temples and megaliths around the globe that ancient man did understand the procession and movements of the planets. Only by understanding the Earth to be round would ancient man have been able to predict, map, and show the wonders of the heavens as some god like deity shining down on us.

2   Genesis 1:9, "And god said, "Let the water under the sky be gathered into one place, and let dry ground appear." He called this dry ground, Land, and the water, Sea."

Now, amazingly, we find scientists in the form of Geologists, backing up this remarkable ancient writing. They say that at one time in the Earth's history there must have been one landmass, which by forces below the surface crust, was moved apart. This has been shown with various strata in all the continents of earth, in their correct positions, matching up. We can even buy an encyclopaedia on CD which shows us this action in slow motion.

On it's own; this evidence could be taken as coincidence. If all the other pieces of evidence stand up, then it can be used as an additional piece of evidence on behalf of the Christians, Jews and Muslims. However, all the other evidence being in jeopardy and that there are so many other rational explanations, then this must be taken as a non-critical piece of evidence.

3   Revelation 21:1, "Then I saw a new Heaven and a new Earth, for the first Heaven and the first Earth had passed away..."

Christians point to the evidence those Scientists now state that one day there will be a big crunch, when the Universe stops expanding and actually contracts. In fact they say it will start all over again and we will get a "new Heaven and a new Earth."

4   People argue against miracles, suggesting they break the Law of Nature. This can be a major problem for Christians. However we must here state their argument. Firstly, they say, who wrote the Laws of Nature? Secondly, as man breaks his own rules, so then god is entitled to break the foolish rules of those creatures it is claimed he created. Thirdly, next time you see the sunrise or a rainbow cross the sky then you have seen a miracle. Right.

Firstly, the Laws of Nature, have been discovered, not written by man. They are elementary mathematical equations discovered to exist within the structure of existence. Secondly, what kind of all knowing god breaks any rules anyway? Thirdly, sun rising and rainbows are natural phenomena which man has attributed to god for thousands of years. We now know exactly what these are and can explain them using good scientific methodology.

5   Scientists tell us that all they can see of the whole universe is 1%, leaving 99% unseen by the human eye.

Hebrews 11:3 states, "By faith we understand that the Universe was formed at God's command, so that what is seen was not made out of what was visible." Therefore, we cannot see that which made us and that which made us was? Yep you guessed it, god. It's not really proof though; it's fairly obvious.

6   The Theory of Quantum Physics states that invisible energy holds all things together. Colossians 1:17, "He is before all things, and in him all things holds together." Christ was in the beginning and through him all things were made. Could this be the 'god' particle that scientists are searching for? This was a fairly well developed philosophy at the time. The Greeks were excellent and we must point out, Pagan, exponents of such ideas. It is now well known that many of these New Testament ideas came from the Hellenised world. So, if it wasn't god's idea, then it

cannot be claimed as proof. Although Christians will point out that, however god managed to get the information to the early Christians doesn't matter, the information got there because god made sure it did.

7   In Joshua 10:12 we find that "the sun stood still". This is an obvious problem scientifically. The sun cannot stand still. However, we do find some remarkable claims from the Christians here. Herodotus the historian claims Egyptian priests revealed to him records of an unusually long day. The Hindu scriptures say, "In the life of Chrishnu, the sun delayed setting to hear the pious ejaculations of Akroon." Again, similar things are found in folklore around the globe. So much so that one must ask the question was there some great worldwide spectacle, such as a comet coming close to Earth and lighting up the sky for an extended period of time. Much like the universal flood, the archetypal elemental memory of this seems to have extended into the folklore of the world. I must here state that it is my belief, based upon a lot more evidence than this, that folklore does always begin in truth somewhere and like Chinese whispers increases in strength and fervour as time goes by.

There have been several scientific explanations that have been put forward, such as eclipses, transits and equinoxes with some extraordinarily big named scientists backing them, which in itself shows that even scientists take this element of the Bible seriously.

Conclusion

The foregoing argument by no means expends every scientific argument made by Christians, or for that matter every argument used by atheists against Christianity. It does not even scratch the surface; however, these are the strongest of the arguments.

Some of us sit back and comprehend this life as if it were an accident of nature. Others seek the truth as if truth needed an explanation, which included god. Christians say that science reveals the magic and wonder of god, a true sight into the creation of god. But when we have this belief taken away we are depressed and saddened.

An incidental component which must be brought to light is the fact that no other religion on Earth except Christianity has anything akin to the scientific back up that Christians point to. The reason for this is simple. Many of the other religions understand that their belief is built upon faith. Facts simply do not matter. Even deeper than this are the Gnostics (gnosis = knowledge). These are searchers after truth, within each religion. Unlike the literal elements of the faith, the Gnostics do not attempt to create or even follow dogma and doctrine. They learn from the Gnostics of other faiths, without the need for physical violence. This is where religion has, in my opinion, gone wrong. It finds the need to structure; document and force-feed controlling doctrine upon the masses. In fact the truth behind each religion is indeed the same thing and this is why people such as the Templars and the Assassins got on so well. They understood the basic Gnostic principles of each other's faiths as being the same thing, personal self-fulfilment.

There have been many scientists follow the age-old pattern of joining in with literal fundamentalists and have stated their faith in this religion or that. There are many Christian scientists, many Islamic and Judaic scientists. Surely, we are asked, if even these, once sceptical people, can openly state their new beliefs in god then what about us. But would it make us happier to state a belief and then follow the rulebook? Or would we be happier following a path towards enlightenment? That is, towards our own understanding of ourselves in relation to the universe.

It is true that scientists are human too, and have emotions just like the rest of us. We are told that when they were confronted with the big bang theory they reacted strongly, refusing to admit god. One scientist saying "it cannot really be true.", another stating that "the notion of a beginning is repugnant to me." This is equally as bad as Christians refusing to alter their mind set on the literal truths behind the Bible. And this is where the fundamental problem between Christianity and science lies. Structures and rules have been incorrectly added into an emotional and very human struggle and search for truth. Then with science, even more factual structures and rules are 'discovered' and the rule books conflict. Had Christianity been less strict about stating the literal truth of the Gospel then it would have stood a better chance for survival and would have adopted the scientific way rather than rejected it.

Maybe we should take a fresh look and understand that science and the Bible need not conflict. In the end, we are no nearer the proof we are looking for. We are, however, building up the picture.

Creative Evolution

What is meant by the word evolution? Simply, it claims that quite naturally, living creatures have changed over the course of millions of years, without the intervention of a divine being, and that we all came from a single celled ancestor, emerging from the waters of an age old sea or cascading down upon our plant from the sky in the form of bacteria.

The problem with this for Christians is that they believe god created everything as specific species. This is the clear statement of the Bible laid out in Genesis. In essence it means that an elephant has always been an elephant and has never been a frog anywhere in it's ancestral lineage.

A small point must first be made before carrying headlong. The word species, as used in the Bible, has and can be used by people, to have different meanings. Some would have us believe that dogs have evolved into all manners of distinct species. This however is blatantly not true, as no matter which dog we look at, be it Alsatian or Poodle, it is still of the species dog.

In the early part of the last century Professor William Bateson defined species as a group of organisms with alike characteristics and freely interbreeding. To prove this point many scientists attempted crossing species to see if they had named them correctly. For an example they crossed the horse and donkey only to find that the result was eventually a completely sterile mule, which either looked like a horse or a donkey. Occasionally this mule would be fertile (only in rare females), but it's offspring always reverted back to the original species of horse or donkey. Consequently a horse was a horse and a donkey was a donkey, two distinct species.

So what did this mean to the poor old dog? Well should a dog mate with another breed of dog the result would be a fertile mongrel which was obviously a dog. However, should the dog try to breed with a cat there would be no result as they are separate species. So, as Christians point out, the animals were created after their kind, they were not meant to interbreed with each other. Now, however, modern day genetic god play is having serious consequences on this idea. This modern scientific idea of playing god trying to cross species genetically is having serious implications for the Christians. So far, geneticists have failed to correctly cross species, but it is only a matter of time. They have hybrids, but they are either sterile, die young or are susceptible to all kinds of diseases.

The one question which evolution does not answer at all is how did this remarkable thing called life get here? It can give us its opinion on how man emerged from the primordial soup, but it cannot tell us who put the primordial soup there in the first place.

For evolutionists to say that life arrived by spontaneous generation is not acceptable to the human mind. They must answer the whole question.

So what is spontaneous generation? Some evolutionists pointed to how, when water was left standing, small organisms would soon erupt into life spontaneously. However in 1846 Pasteur demonstrated that bacteria did not originate of it's own accord, but from other bacteria which was already in place in the water.

Pasteur proved that all living things do and have come from other living things and therefore living things must have been created in the first place (or at least the 4 building blocks to life in RNA must have been placed carefully in the right place at just the right time). Even Charles Darwin once said, "I imagine that probably all organic beings which ever lived on this earth descended from some primitive form, which was first called, into life by the creator."

So at the first hurdle evolution supposedly falls. It cannot explain the origin of species at all, just theorise imaginatively about change. It does not give us the answer to how it originated.

Let us now look at a few evolutionary proofs or theories.

Related Anatomy

This is the study of physical resemblances throughout nature. The similarity between bone structure, muscular forms and nerves.

Evolutionists believe that by comparing the anatomies of animals, which are alive today with humans, or other animals they can show the links between the various affinities. For instance, two eyes, legs and arms of the ape against two eyes, legs and arms of the human.

However, this simple comparing is no proof for evolution or creation alike. It still requires faith in the chosen doctrine as any evidence is purely inference and not fact. Creationists see in Related Anatomy the same general plan of the creator. After all, why make one perfect blue print and then start all over again? We all live on the same planet, breath the same air, live under the same sun and drink the same fluid, water. Therefore we must be similar in certain aspects, just as the creator made us? Or just as evolution naturally uses the same chemicals and environment to build us?

Christians say they need not deny the similar attributes, but admit them and show them equally as evidence for creation. Did god vary the DNA pattern of life? Making us so much alike, yet unusually different in so many incompatible ways?

Evolutionists are now unable to decide whether species x came from family tree a or b, or whether they have named the species incorrectly. For instance, take dolphins, whales and porpoises. If one side of evolution is to be believed then these three kinds of creatures are fish, as they more closely resemble those aquatic, cold blooded animals. They must have evolved from the same line as fish. However, they are mammals like us. They do not lay eggs; they are warm-blooded and suckle their young. Therefore, they must have evolved from land mammals as well as fish. Obviously this is impossible, so what is the truth? Is it that they evolved from hoofed land mammals, more likely the swine as some evolutionists believe? Or fish? The answer, for Christians, is in Genesis 1:21, "So God created the great creatures of the sea and every living and moving thing with which the water teems, according to their kinds..."

Vestigial Organs

It is said by the evolutionist that there are certain organs and glands within the body of man that are now of no use. Once, in the ascent of mankind (maybe as a pig or something), these organs were used, but now as we have evolved we have kept them as merely fillers of spaces.

A few of these so-called vestigial organs in man are the thyroid glands, the tonsils, the thymus gland, the pituitary gland, the vermiform appendix and the pineal gland.

Evolutionists jumped on this proof with added fervour, shouting gloriously that we all had organs with which we could dispense.

Sadly though this list of useless body parts has been diminished as our knowledge has expanded. Now we know that all these organs are useful. For one example the thyroid gland we know controls the Iodine in the food we eat.

Geology

This is the study of the strata of rock layers around the globe. The geologist says that the layers at the bottom were deposited first and the ones above subsequently in order or time. This depositing of layers according to them took millions of years.

If this, and evolution, is correct then we should be able to see a unique record of the ascent of man, from the single celled amoeba to Homo Sapiens Sapiens, in fossil record. That, the further down we dig, the further down the evolutionary tree we climb.

However, if this is the case, why did Dr M. Pickford when writing in the New Scientist say, "The fossil void is particularly frustrating."?

He said this for the simple reason that there are almost no links of fact and more links of faith.

There are no reptiles with scales gradually turning into feathers or fur. No mice with half wing and half leg on it's merry way towards becoming a bat and no pig running into the water wanting to be a whale. When we look at the vision of a missing link we must realise that we are actually looking for millions upon millions of missing links between all living things. We have not found one, and there should be millions.

Unfortunately these links are simply non-existent. Indeed, the gaps are so broad that no evolutionary line can be arranged at all without guesswork.

In fact, forms of man and animals go back a long way in fossil evidence quite unaltered. Species have died out, and new ones emerged, but there are few definitive half way marks.

Lets look at an example. In 1938 in South Africa fishermen brought to the surface a five-foot long fish, weighing 27 pounds. Strangely this fish could only be given the title Coelacanth and is the exact replica of it's fossilised ancestor of the same name.

This ancestor is said to have become extinct in the Triassic age, some 90 million years ago. The fish had not altered at all. Why? There have since been found Coelacanths all around the coast. Some have slight variations in size and colour due to the depth of water and the environment in which they live. But, in 90 million years they have not turned drastically into Crocodiles or developed language and built underground houses. They have happily unaltered.

Evidence like this has baffled evolutionists ever since Darwin, who himself said, "Geology assuredly does not reveal any such fine graded organic chain." It does not mean that we will not find fossils one day, which substantiate the claims, it just means we have not yet and we need to use the evidence we actually have to make our judgements.

The best geological assumption is that certain fossils are older than others, and by this proof they claim for instance that reptiles pre-date horses and therefore horses evolved from reptiles.

However, again it is a theory with no hard evidence. Horses may well have roamed around one part of the planet whilst reptiles ruled another. There is no evidence to the contrary, just a stated belief. Indeed, one eminent scientist in America once stated that there might have been mammals in the Palaeozoic era. It is even now an evolutionary theory that man may after all have lived alongside the dinosaurs. It would be a re-writing of the evolutionary history books if either of these was found to be true, showing that the last hundred years of evolutionary ideology was flawed.

The method employed in the ageing of fossil evidence is at best doubtable. It seems that when geologists finds a strata of rock with certain deposits of animal forms, he takes it to the evolutionist who dates it according to the evolutionary theory! If then the geologist goes away and finds a higher form of life within the same strata he must run back and have it re-dated. In defence of the poor old creationist, if he were to have his rocks labelled according to the whim of theory then he would be accused of manipulating the facts. Dating should come with a warning on the bottle - these dates are assumed and not factual. As it is, the world is told an assumption as if it were an actuality, which would not be a problem if it were admitted, but it isn't. We are told that the age of fossil evidence is known; that evolution is scientifically proven. We are in fact far from knowing these things scientifically.

It is in the same vein that scientists play with the order of fossil evidence. They claim, quite believably, that the simplest forms of life were first and the more complex forms after. The most complex forms evolved out of the simplest forms and therefore the simplest forms ought to be found on the lower strata geological levels. However, this is not always the case. The simpler forms of life are not always found on the bottom layers. The order of evolutionary events is often found to be upside down. This has thrown the scientists into a high state of drama with some new and radical theories. These upside down areas are known across the globe, from the Alps to Scotland, from New York to Norway, in many instances for thousands of miles.

So what do our evolutionary inclined scientists claim for an explanation? It appears by a miracle of nature that some way the earth's crust slid, flipped over and then the layers rested perfectly horizontally, bottom on top and top on bottom.

These are called faults, as if the earth were to blame somehow for falsifying the evidence. It should at this stage be pointed out that geologists have as yet, found no real reason or evidence that this actually happened, but rest assured, they will soon have a theory. Nobody will put their hands up and say that maybe the evidence is right and we have to rethink our theories regarding gradual evolution.

Geology and its time-scales of millions of years are built on the evolutionist's theories. The Earth is made to conform to Darwinist theories and compelled to be at fault if it does not.

Fossil evidence of links between marsupials and mammals, reptiles and fishes and all living things is non-existent and based upon theories. The evidence simply proves that species have never altered, they may have died out and new ones emerged, but they did not alter into other species. What the evidence does suggest is another theory. That great catastrophe, natural occurrences or some other action caused life to change, and change virtually overnight. Maybe disease, brought about by flooding, draughts, earthquakes or volcanic eruptions, causes some biological and genetic reaction which within the space of one or two generations brings about drastic species altering change and that some of these new genetically altered species survive the new conditions better than others and natural selection becomes evident. This then, is the new theory that evolutionists are turning to more and more. Indeed, even Professor Fred Hoyle spoke about the evidence actually being in contradiction to Darwin's theory, however Darwin did not evade problems with gradual evolution. Neo-Darwinism accepts this new radical change theory.

Changes

There are countless explanatory theories on how species have altered. Some are in the realm of Alice's Wonderland. Others are more subtle, easy to believe and yet still quite profoundly, theories.

The French evolutionist, Lamarck, was the originator of one of the most romantic and enduring theories. He believed that if a blacksmith were to constantly use his arm, then it would develop a larger and larger muscle. This is blatantly true, which is always a good leader into a theory as it lends an element of truth to the thesis. Consequently, said Lamarck, if this were carried on generation after generation then we would have a race of big armed blacksmiths. The same notion was applied as evidence for the evolution of the animal kingdom. Take the Flamingo, with his long spindly legs. Lamarck insisted that it's ancestors had short legs, but by continual effort over thousands of years to walk in water and get food without wetting it's feathers the short legs became longer and longer.

If you have not yet laughed yourself to death then just consider the following: -

Where are all the fossils of short and medium length Flamingo legs?
Why did it not evolve the capacity to swim?
Why did it not evolve to eat different food?
Surely, waiting thousands of years for your collective legs to grow would have starved Flamingo's and there would no longer be any Flamingo's left?
Why did the other birds not also develop long legs?
Indeed, why didn't the Flamingo turn into a Duck?

What of our poor old blacksmith? It is a plain fact that no matter how much we increase the size of our muscles, our offspring will come out according to our DNA pattern and not our work pattern. For thousands of years we have spoken languages. Yet our children still have to be taught from birth. They are not born with the ability to talk. We have been cutting off our hair for as long as there have been hair salons, and yet it still grows in each generation. The Jews have been circumcising for over 4000 years and yet their foreskin still grows on their offspring. Chinese women for countless generations have bound their feet, yet when allowed to grow, they grow normally. There can be obvious genetic traits shown, such as skin colour, which do alter according to environmental specifications, but our legs do not grow or arms bulge to the extent that Lamarck was insinuating.

Certainly if gradual evolution were correct all these things would by now have had some affect upon us, however small.

The final nail in Lamarck's coffin was science itself, which seemed to side with god. We are told that there are two types of cells, which make up the individual. The body cell and the germ cell. In the beginning of our lives the germ cells are set aside and the body cells allowed to take over, providing our growth. Now the only time that these germ cells come into action again is at our reproductive stage when they are used to pass on information to the next generation. Therefore, no matter what we do to our body during our lives, whether be a blacksmith or imitate a Flamingo, we will never pass our developed traits on to our children, only our inherent ones. Environmental effects are a different matter entirely. This of course, backs up the Christian argument. The Bible says that life and species are within the seed, which is now being shown to be true via science.

The same thing, however, also applies to Darwin's theory of natural selection. However, more than that, he fails to give us any guidance on just how the species came into existence in the first instance. As Professor Lock of Cambridge University once said, "Selection, whether natural or artificial, can have no power in creating anything new."

Natural selection it seems may explain the survival of the fittest, but it does not yet explain the arrival of the fittest.

Darwin himself said if it could be demonstrated that any complex organ existed and had arrived not by numerous alterations, then this theory would break down completely.

Could it be that all creatures have arrived without numerous alterations? Take as demonstration the bat. This tiny creature is said to have evolved from something akin to the mouse. Supposing for one moment that the mouse had actually spent thousands of years running along, jumping in the air, in the vain hope that one day it would fly, and supposing that wings did begin to sprout. We would then have a mouse with half a leg and half a wing. How would it cope? How could we possibly say that it was the fittest of the species when encumbered with a deformity like this? Apart from obvious such reasoning we have to ask our evolutionist for one piece of evidence, a fossil. There has not been one fossil found to back up Lamarck's gradual evolution theories. And yet many still believe them.

From the position of requiring evidence for the existence of god, I have to ask a reverse question. Where is the evidence for evolution? It seems to be almost non-existent, if it were not for the strong theoretical and almost common sense element of the argument.

So what did the great Darwin, that changer of mans mind, really think? Well it is actually a documented fact that he held mission conversions on his lawn, converting people to Christianity! He also made regular donations to South American Missionaries. When confronted with the lack of fossil evidence he had no other explanation than special creation. At the end of his life he exclaimed his regret for the use of his theory by Karl Marx against god and the subsequent results that this had on mankind. In fact, some of his very last words were, "How I wish I had not expressed my theory of evolution as I have done."

The world, however, seems to disregard this and still holds to Darwinist theories, but now include a subtle blend of mutation factors. These however, are still changing as Darwin's theories have done.

All we can do is sit back and wait for science to come up with a better factual based theory than we presently possess, as the present theory has to many flaws.

The Christian theology on the subject can be simplified as follows: -

God created all living things, placing in each one a certain number of genes, which, like any piano, only has a certain number of notes, and can only play a certain number of chords. We can see this in many varied kinds of the human races. This factor inhibits species x to stay as species x and to not move beyond the limits set by god in his DNA coding sequence, patented to Heaven Inc. Therefore the only changes allowed are those god allows in his coding.

Of course the argument is that the coding is a complex system brought about by the unique cosmic mix presented in our ancient universe. It is one way or another, a fantastic natural phenomena that we have not yet thoroughly explained from the available evidence. In short, our theories are in need of fact or our facts are in need of a new theory.

Did man come from the ape?

The evolutionists point at the ape and say, "Don't we look like that? We must have come from it." To which the creationist response goes, "No, we did not come from that, but maybe you inherited it's brains." (Of course, I in now way wish to insult apes.)

The Christians are here fighting a losing battle. Although the current factual evidence is extremely poor, the financial might of the scientists will prevail and find new evidence. However, the following is the argument given by the Christians.

Firstly, where did the ape come from? Man has twelve pairs of ribs. The gorilla has thirteen. The gibbon has arms that touch the floor and thirteen pairs of ribs. All apes have four 'hands'; their feet have a thumb, not a big toe. Secondly, the most startling proof that I have found was the lack of evidence for the so-called, 'Evolution of Man' image.

This is the best piece of evolutionary propaganda on the market. A useful, imaginative, visual aid to inspiring worldwide belief. This most simple of hypnotic devices has spellbound several generations and is touted in schools across the globe, subtly brainwashing (Christians belief) our children into a supposedly non-existent proof. We have all seen it, that picture of a stooping ape, gradually altering in each successive picture until eventually he stands completely upright and becomes man. Many believe this picture as if it is actual proof in itself. It is a convincing image of a 'theory'. It is not a reflection of the evidence, but a simple visual aid of the theoretical result of the evidence to hand. Many scientists will admit that there is no fossil data to back this myth up at all. It is not just the notion that there are far too few links between ape and man been discovered in fossil evidence. It is the simple facts that there is no fossil evidence of any of the links. In fact, we could simply put all the fossil skeletons we have in a big box, shuffle them up and put them back together again as modern man. Many of the skeletons have been arranged with a pre-conceived idea that they should stoop. After a hard day at work, I too stoop.

Of the missing links, which at one time were held up as proof by some scientists, only a few are worth considering here. Pithecanthropus was a myth created by a French man called Dubois. He fooled the establishment for many years with his dreadful fake. One Professor exclaimed, "We do not even know whether he (Dubois) told the truth about the remains or not." This young evolutionist went out with the full intention of recovering the missing link. All he found was a mixture of human and ape like remains, from separate sites, which were then carefully manipulated and falsified and exclaimed as being the missing link. This missing link is now missing from the science textbook.

Perhaps one of the most famous proofs is the Neanderthalenis or Neanderthal Man. Regardless of what is claimed for these particular skeletal remains, creationists actually claim Neanderthal as evidence that man has not altered at all!

He was originally found by two workmen who carelessly dug him up and lost many vital parts, leaving only the skull and a few minor bones. One big surprise is his brain capacity, which is the standard of any European today at 1330 cubic centimetres. It is a remarkable observation, that if we should dress up our Neanderthal in modern clothes and set him off walking down any high street in any town then you would be under a very great challenge to point him out amongst the crowd. He would not look unusual; in fact many of our modern citizens look distinctly more peculiar.

Of all the Neanderthals found to date we can safely conclude that they would pass to be fully human dressed in flesh and sinew, with a covering of skin and a Burton suite. Indeed the brain capacity of the La Chappelle-aux-Saints skull is 1600 cc.

The same is almost as true for Cro-Magnon. Again, he is like any other modern day man. However this time evolutionists use the supra-orbital bone to prove that he cannot be fully human and looks more like what we perceive he should look like, as a staging post between ape and man. On closer investigation I have myself found between 10-20% of the people I came into contact with on one particular day to have this supra-orbital structure. Not very scientific, and not a huge market test. But then, we only have a dozen or so skeletons to base our theories on as well. Cro-Magnons brain capacity is on a par, if not superior to modern man and again if we force the image into a full upright position, clothe him in an England football shirt then we have somebody we would not look twice at in the street.

All we have to do is recognise that not every bone we dig up is going to be a six foot, white, Aryan and standard European, who roamed around with a club in hand looking for a Mammoth to turn into burgers. Take a look around you, at the variations in skin, bone structure and size the next time you are out. You will see tall, thin, fat, beautiful, ugly, and any number of them could, if we use our current methodology, be perceived as the missing link. The true natural history of man is still, itself, missing, and this link needs to be discovered if we are to squash the arguments.

One of the problems we have pointed out is the preconceived idea that many evolutionists have when searching for evidence. An example utilised by the Christians is mineralised bones, where evolutionists maintained that if a bone became mineralised then it was very old. A human bone buried in a moist environment will become seriously mineralised in a relatively short time. If the remains of stone implements are found with the bones of man, then it is said to be from the Stone Age. This, however, might not necessarily be the case. Even today, in the twenty-first century, there are tribes around the globe using stone tools. It is not a perfect and exact method of ageing.

There are other examples which are quite startling if we should draw the conclusion from the evidence, rather than from theory.

Take for instance the Table Top Mountain peculiarity. Table Top Mountain is in California on the western realm of Yosemite National Park. The top of this mountain is made up of a 9 million year old lava cap. Beneath are gold gravels, lying just above the ancient bedrock. Many mines were dug into this rock in the search for gold and it was during this search that many ancient artefacts were uncovered within the prehistoric gravel. Spear heads, bow handles, stone grinding tools, ladles with handles and a human jaw bone. Strangely, this layer of gravel has been dated to between 33 to 55 million years old. Many other items were discovered, among them a bead of white marble about one and a half inches long with a hole drilled right through it. Between 1869 and 1877 Clarence King, a professional geologist also discovered items which were simply 'in the wrong place', including a stone pestle wedged deep within that hard gravel. Table Top Mountain is not the only sight to have brought up such finds however.

One anthropologist, commissioned by the University of California to destroy the beliefs beginning to surround these discoveries said "It would necessitate placing the origin of the human race in an exceedingly remote geological period. This is contrary to all precedent in the history of organisms, which teaches that mammalian species are short lived."

If we remember that man is supposed to have evolved from the primates some 3-5 million years ago, then this resultant evidence, factual evidence, not theory, is not consistent. It seems that evolution needs looking at again and re-dating, or answers needs to be given to the questions that arise out of such discoveries, answers that are not based around previous pre-conceived theories.

However, just because the evolutionists do have preconceived ideas before they even start, so do Christians, the same Christians that simply will not alter their opinion, regardless of evidence. So we have to ask ourselves, no matter what evidence is found, will it ever be good enough?

6   DNA

Deoxyribonucleic Acid, or commonly known as DNA. This fantastic information model is an incredibly complex base part of every living being. It designates what we will be, not who we will be. At present this very essential part of life is being broken down and sold off around the world to international chemical and biological organisations who are patenting the very Bible of life as if they invented it. But why do Christians use this very scientific element as proof for the existence of god?

Biblically the seed is passed on from one person to their offspring from generation to generation (Genesis 3:15).

DNA is the same as the germ seed we previously discussed and is passed on as the Biblical seed states.

Biblically Eve (Hawah) was the mother of all who live (genesis 3:20). Christians point this out, especially now as scientists claim to have proven that via DNA research all mankind came from one mother. In fact they have said a couple. Anthropologists have traced this DNA clue right back to the Euphrates; the same place archaeologists have traced back the origins of farming. It is attributed to a plateau in the highlands of western Turkey, which is the source of the four rivers, the Pison, Gihon, Tigris and Euphrates. They have found a succession of pottery, pollen core samples and local dry farming techniques, which match the ideas of migrating man. Genesis 2:10 says, "A river watering the Garden flowed from Eden; from there it was separated into four headwaters." These headwaters were the rivers Pison, Gihon, Tigris and Euphrates. Eden means plateau. Jungian archetypes and collective consciousness could have a play here in the ancient belief of the Garden of Eden, but the scientific patterns are remarkably close to the Biblical, and other Mesopotamian, texts.

DNA is in all living things. Christians ask where did it come from? The code, they say, is so complicated that it would take more than a million pages of instructions for us to understand it. DNA, therefore, the Christians exclaim, must have existed for life to be. It is a fundamental part of life, yet we do not known where such a thing came from. Did it occur by mutation, or accident? Even scientists are as yet unsure. The Christians believe that DNA simply had to have been made. The chances of such a complicated and perfect mathematical chemical pattern to have appeared by accident is beyond their Biblical reasoning powers. There had to be life for there to be DNA and there had to be DNA for there to be life. Chicken and Egg.

This, at present, seems to be a stalemate. Until new evidence or a contrary theory erupts, we have no answer. It may simply be a possibility for the whole thing, with the right amount of time and the right environmental conditions, to have evolved on a lower level, before mutational events occurred, causing radioactive alterations to the basic DNA structure. But then I am not a biologist and we must wait and see.

Conclusion

So, what can we deduce from all the above? Firstly, we can see that even from such a small selection of the argument there is a lot of controversy, even now, when we are told the modern age is here and we must have faith in science. There are still flaws; it is still a relatively young human belief. Religion, faith and belief have, after all, been around a lot longer than our modern scientific version. We see that there are some startling statements from science, which are just theories and that these theories are linked to some flawed evidence.

In related anatomy we see an evolutionary scientist struggling and grasping at straws to prove his faith. What he misses, according to Christians, is the simple fact that it does not matter if things look the same, maybe they were created that way?

His own experiments and investigations then help to kill the vestigial organs proof for evolution. In geology we find some peculiar dating techniques which need strengthening if they are to be taken as total proof. Again, in the imagery of the stooping ape we are to be convinced like some mass marketed consumer wishing to buy in on the evolutionary angle. Evidence is virtually non-existent and there are many blatant lies and cover-ups.

Christians tell us that we are struggling to disprove the simple truth of a creating god. It could be that our brains are at fault, and that we are hoping that we have developed further than we actually have. When we force our poor old brain to struggle with the immense complexities of an ex-chaotic and beautifully mathematical universe, with quantum physics and elementary particle physics confusing us even more, we simply give in and believe the most understandable, which today is evolution. Two thousand years ago is was creation.

We must question everything then. Every time a scientist explains a new theory, remember that word, theory. The next time a preacher tries to tell you that a creating god moulded man out of clay, remember that other word, theology. They are the same things.

At the end of the day, you have to decide whether the evidence convinces you, and what it convinces you of. The Bible does not have to be literally correct; it can be seen as a wonderful Gnostic text, giving insight and enlightenment. It could be the result of many hundreds of years of wisdom, which is there to tell us why. Science with its technical and factual approach should be strictly for telling us how. We could split the two elements into why and how. We could, if we were happy to. Are you happy to?

Notes:

Fossil evidence - forbidden.

The fossil evidence of early man is remarkably in complete contrast to current theory. If we are to take into account the actual evidence then we revert to an early man being from extreme antiquity. In 1922 a mining engineer found a remarkable footprint in Nevada. This the clearly defined sole of a shoe! Showing fine stitching and an indentation in the sole which could only have been caused by wear.

The fossil was taken to geologists from Columbia University and three professors of the American Museum of Natural History. All stated and agreed that the fossil evidence came from the Triassic period, over 213 million years ago. They claimed, however, that it must be a freak. And yet, experts from the Rockafeller Institute produced microscopic analysis which showed that the twists of the thread in the fossil simply must be real. The Fossil disappeared and today will not be found in any textbook.

A second shoe print was found in 1968 when William Meister split open a 505 million year old shale to reveal a sandal print over ten inches long. Under the shoe print was a Trilobite, crushed by the sandal. A second Trilobite had crawled into the heal indentation and was also clearly fossilised at the same time as the sandal print. A creature extinct for millions of years, found above and below the sandal print of a human. How is this possible? Either our dating of the fossil records is out by millions of years or man has walked the planet, in shoes, for much longer than current theory. (A third option would be time travel from the future - but our current 'theory' does not allow for this to happen). This is evidence, swept aside by our experts because it does not fit their theory, shame we are not allowed to decide for ourselves, rather than have evidence like this hidden from us.

God's Abacus

A remarkable discovery by a man called Dr Ivan Panin more than forty years ago now still remains virtually an untold story. Panin was a Russian, living in America. He was a brilliant mathematician, fluent in Hebrew and Greek, and an agnostic. The story goes that out of literary interest he decided to read the Old Testament in its original language. He stumbled upon what he believed to be mathematical proof that god existed.

To make a start we shall take the Hebrew alphabet. This consists of 22 letters with 5 finals added to make up 3 series of 9 or 27 letters in all. Each letter in the alphabet has a number attributed to it. For example, Aleph = 1 and Samech = 60.

Therefore when a word, sentence, paragraph or chapter is written in Hebrew, it also carries a numerical value.

This numerical value in turn has a spiritual coding and when the passage is broken down different spiritual values are found for each saying, word or name. As a few examples I have chosen the more important numbers in the Bible. Number 1 represents the beginning and unity. Number 3 means completeness or fullness. Number 7 is spiritual holiness. Number 12 is the perfection of the governing body or rulers. So we can see that within the very words of the Bible there can be a more subtle meaning or insight.

This is not unusual in itself as Latin also has numbers attributed to its letters. Even the English language has a kind of numerology. For example when we take the numbers that are given to the English language and work out the number for the name Jesus Christ we find that we get the number 7. This is then translated to mean 'the mystery'.

What is striking nevertheless is the ridiculous repetition of the number seven or multiples of seven in the original Hebrew script.

Panin found that in the Hebrew Old Testament there were as many as seventy occurrences of this in every passage. Not only that, but in every possible way that the passage could be divided, including grammatical construction. From passage to passage there was an amazing over-arching link of septenary design, which carried on and on throughout the whole of a single book. Also when all the books are put together as one the same remarkable link occurs, as if they were somehow meant to be together. Every passage of every book, and every book of the Old Testament has this design. Nothing seems to upsets its course, not even the long lists of names which sometimes can be laborious.

Getting back to numbers, we find that in each passage there is anything from 12 to 100 features of this design.

To elucidate the impossibility of this occurrence we shall take the possibility of there being only 24 features in one passage, of one book. The stunning mathematical chance is 1 over 191581231380566414000.

This is just the chance of it happening once for a 24-feature passage. Please remember that this occurs throughout the Old Testament, sometimes with 100 features. The chance of this is more than could be written on all the paper in the world. Dr Panin and two expert mathematicians spent thirteen weeks trying to write just one passage with just seven features. Surely, if these men, with all their knowledge could not re-create the structure then we are faced with a very peculiar phenomenon. The three experts failed, utterly.

What about the New Testament of the Christians?

This, the second part of the Bible was written in mainly Greek. The alphabet, correspondingly also has numbers attributed to them. For instance, Alpha = 1 and Upsilon = 400. Therefore, maybe it too has some kind of a design? It does. It is exactly the same as the Old Testament.
But don't take just my word for it; let's look at Mark as an example.

In the last twelve verses alone there are 60 features. A few as follows; 175 words or 25 x 7; 98 words or 2 x 7 x 7; 553 letters or 79 x 7; 133 forms or 19 x 7. This carries on and on throughout the whole of the New Testament unbroken.

It may also be of note that in English there is a strange medieval numerology. This works by writing the numbers 1 to 9 across and the subsequently the English alphabet underneath as follows.
1 2 3 4 5 6 7 8 9
A B C D E F G H I
J K L M N O P Q R
S T U V W X Y Z

If we write 'Jesus Christ' in numbers, 15131 389912, it equals the total 43, which we then add together to get the final total which is 7. Again, as in the Hebrew and Greek, the English numbers have meanings.

The number 7 means mysterious and austere. Of course this is just a coincidental analysis, discovered purely whilst investigating numerology and no proof for the Bible is accepted from it. (See notes end of chapter).

Have you been branded with the number of the beast?

The idea that we will all have the number of the beast tattooed on our hands or foreheads has been around for a long time and there are many theories from the Christians as to how this will be done. Microchip implants being one of the latest. The humble bar code has been abused in this area. The universally accepted form of pricing and itemising has come under the watchful eye of our friendly evangelist. The EAN 13 International Bar Code has 13 digits (13 is bad if you're a Christian). The following is an example of how we constantly get 666 out of our bar codes.

Every bar code has three taller bars, one at the start, one in the middle and one at the end. This bar is 6, so all bar codes have 666 on them.
630 nanometers = 630 divided by 6 = 105 = 1+0+5 = 6 = 666.
630 nanometers = 630 = 6+3+0 = 9. 9 divided by 3 = 3 or 3 sixes.
630 nanometers = 6 x 3 = 9 divided by 3 = 3 (add all up = 24 = 2 + 4 = 6.
Each module or bar is equal width. This nominal width is .33mm. There are 7 modules.
= 7 x .33 = 231 = 2 + 3 + 1 = 6
= 3 + 3 x 7 = 42 = 4 + 2 = 6
+ 2 sections of 6 = 666
or 3 x 7 = 21 = 2 + 1 = 3 x 2 sections of 6 = 666
Numerology - the Bibles number system, a second level cipher coding system built up over hundreds of years.

Conclusion

I am not going to lead you anywhere with this evidence. It is the last such chapter in this book and I have purposely decided that this is the strongest evidence we have to hand. It should, therefore, be perused, investigated and decided upon by the searching element of your conscious, bearing in mind all that has been said before.

Notes on Sevens

Sevens. Joshua walked around Jericho (the first civilisation according to some and home of the largest group of Shamans) seven times.

Seven heavens - Koran, Bible, Shaman, Druids.

Seven deadly sins and seven virtues.

Life has seven cycles according to tradition.

Seven steps to Heaven, popular belief and on ziggurats.

The seventh son of the seventh son is by Jewish tradition believed to have great healing powers.

Magic boots, that allow the wearer to walk seven leagues in one stride, goes back to the mythical magic of the giants or men of renown.

Seven days in a week, days in creation.

Hebrew to swear on oath means to come under the influence of the seven (probably planets).

The seven Argive heroes of Greek legend.

The seven champions of English legend.

Seven gifts of the spirits.

Seven Japanese gods of Luck.

Seven joys/sorrows of Mary, seven sacraments.

Seven sages of Greece or Wise Men of Greece.

Seven sciences.

Seven senses - according to the ancients. They are under the influence of the planets. Fire moves, earth sense of feeling, water gives speech, air taste, mist sight, flowers hearing and the south wind smell.

Seven Wonders of the ancient world.

Meanings of seven - scholarly, mystical, withdrawn, dreamy, time, the colours of the rainbow, seven tones of the musical scale, stability and endurance, duration.

Numerology has Jesus Christ as the number seven. Septenary design as 777 (the beast 666)

There are seven elementary hues to the spectrum when blended together they form White.

Conclusion

So just what have we seen? Have we seen proof for the existence of a god?

1   The world's prophets and astrologers are doing a good job at self preservation, but relatively little for our souls, and sadly the Bible seems to be no clearer on the subject.

2   There are many religions. To us in this western world, Christianity is the chosen course for spiritual fulfilment, for many reasons. And yet we do not have the real Christianity of the Gnostics, which has been hidden and virtually destroyed by literalist Paulician Christianity.

3   Evolution too is a religion, but an ever changing and developing one. While these are still theories we must be careful. We must only take factual evidence into account for any theory. Could science and faith work together? All the current evidence could back up the atheist or the Christian.

4   Science, like evolution, needs close scrutiny.

5   Historically the Bible is better than most other religious texts, except the apocryphal and hidden gospels such as the Gospel of Thomas or Mary, which may still hold greater secrets. Believing in the Bible as if it were literal truth is untenable.

6   Nobody has yet worked out the remarkable phenomena of septenary design within the Bible. More mathematical investigation is required.

So now, taking into account all the evidence, either factual or circumstantial, whether philosophical or theological, looking at the witnesses, the written and scientific testimony, what have we proven?

The evidence presented in this book has been presented to twelve good people, as if they were a jury. They were asked to make the decision.

The conclusion was startling. Six women, six men. Three believers in Christianity, four atheists, one Jew, one Muslim, one Buddhist and two agnostics. This may not be most fair jury in the world but it was the best UK cross section statistically available.

In weighing the evidence there were still some questions, which can only be considered to be philosophical and not factual. These questions we believed had to remain unanswered and a verdict drawn.

The verdict was eight for the existence of a Biblical god, three against and one no vote.

The verdict was in. The jury deemed there to be sufficient evidence for the positive verdict. It now remained to sum up and make a judgement.

If it was the case that we have proven beyond reasonable doubt that god exists, then we have no choice but to look at what he is supposedly telling us. In the end though, it is up to each one of us, it is still faith, and no amount of proof will convince us to change our mind.

We will all find out eventually.

For myself, I do not believe in god, of any kind. I purely believe that mankind has a long way to go before he realises and can cope with the psychological void that we have evolved when there is no god. If it helps those millions of people who still believe in god to carry on with their lives then who am I to preach to them the opposite? I would however, be careful to consider that mankind has and will use religion to control people, this I know and believe I have proven in my book The Shining Ones. But men who wish to control masses will always find a way, a method and means. Whether it is television, the Internet or sport.

I wish you luck in your search for your own belief, whatever that may be.

Also available from Radikal by the same author

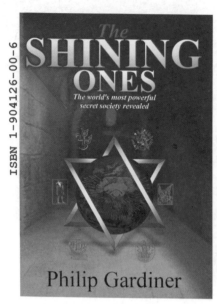

ISBN 1-904126-00-6

Radical author and exponent of truth, Philip Gardiner, has this year stunned the world with these two startling books.

The Shining Ones, an investigation delving back in time thousands of years to reveal an ancient and powerful secret brotherhood. Step aside Graham Hancock, this book alters history.

Where did our god's really come from? Who holds the power? Find out for the first time.

Available from most book stores. However if you have difficulty ordering then call us now on 01773 764288 or you can order online at www.radikalbooks.com.

"exhilarating" "Frightening"
"You will never get this published"
"Turns history upside down"
"Makes you look at the world in a completely different way"